THE
DREAM
FACTORY

THE
DREAM FACTORY

INSIDE THE MAKE-OR-BREAK
WORLD OF FOOTBALL'S ACADEMIES

RYAN BALDI

POLARIS
PUBLISHING

POLARIS PUBLISHING LTD
c/o Aberdein Considine
2nd Floor, Elder House
Multrees Walk
Edinburgh
EH1 3DX

Distributed by Birlinn Limited

www.polarispublishing.com

British Library Cataloguing-in-Publication Data
A catalogue record for this book is available on request from the British Library.

Designed and typeset by Polaris Publishing, Edinburgh
Printed in Great Britain by CPI Group (UK) Ltd, Croydon, CR0 4YY

CONTENTS

For Sophie and Dylan,
my world

LOVE OF THE GAME

THE SILVER THAT flecks the hair at his temples is just about visible from under the woollen hat protecting his head from the chill of this October afternoon. There is little else betraying Tony Whelan's sixty-eight years. He is lean and lithe beneath a thickly-padded gilet embossed with the Manchester United crest. There is an ease to both his movement and his nature. Behind his sepia-brown eyes, there is still, after all these years, a wonderment for his work, a deep reverence for his responsibility.

Whelan, himself a graduate of United's youth system in the late 1960s, has been a coach and mentor to the club's young players since 1990 and assistant academy director since 2005. He has seen the Class of '92 – the gilded generation of Ryan Giggs, David Beckham, Paul Scholes and the Neville brothers – reignite the club's connection to home-bred talent that can be traced back to the Busby Babes. He has helped mould and encourage some of English football's finest prospects to reach the summit of the game, and he has felt powerless as his efforts have failed to prevent an equally gifted few from falling short.

No one over the last three decades has been a more influential presence, a more constant and reliable hand on the tiller, at one of football's most famous and productive youth-development programmes.

Even now, speaking at the tail end of 2020, as the coronavirus pandemic has sent a large portion of United's academy operation into suspended animation, his motivation is undiminished, the joy he finds in his job ever-unbridled. Sitting at a picnic table in the garden area of an upmarket café near Altrincham, a ten-minute drive from the academy – because the pandemic currently prevents him from receiving visitors at the Carrington base – Whelan begins to explain why.

'Love of the game. Love of football,' he says. 'It's always been more than a job.'

Whelan is instantly rhapsodic. He pauses only to take an occasional sip of coffee or to bite a chunk from his chicken sandwich, then he's off again, his passion stirred, his thoughts racing. 'I'm always conscious of the fact that I'm really honoured and privileged to have worked for this club as long as I have done,' he continues. 'I've worked with some wonderful people – managers, coaches and young people. Young people who have inspired me in ways that they don't know and they don't understand. Love of the game has driven me a lot, it has to. What are you getting up in the morning for? I watched football last night, loved every minute of it. I saw some under-11 kids training at Carrington, just coming in buzzing, joyous. Give me some of that. And it's just a great game at the end of the day. That's why I'm such a strong believer in making sure kids love the game. If you love the game, you can still enjoy it at my age. I'm just a couple of years short of seventy now. I still want to be enjoying it in twenty years' time, with any luck.

'As a coach, you want to be challenged. I used to love it when a kid would say, "Tony, why are you doing that? It's rubbish. I want to do this." I'm not saying you let the animals run the zoo, but you have to be open to that. I sometimes think we don't give young people the respect they deserve. We think we know best because we're older than them. I've learned so much from young players, particularly over the last twenty years, just listening, watching, observing.

'When I was involved with the full-time programme, the MANUSS [Manchester United Schoolboy Scholarship] programme, I learned to be a very good observer and a good listener. I became very good at taking the temperature. What are they like today? What is the mood like in the dressing room? What am I going to give them? How am I going to lighten the mood? Are they ready for something really substantial today? And that could change from hour to hour, day to day. That's what I learned. Most of the time, my coaching licences were away in the safe.'

Whelan could retire tomorrow – could have retired ten years ago – and his legacy in the game would stand totemic in the form of the players he has ushered through United's academy. But he understands, perhaps better than anybody, that someone in his position has a greater responsibility than to simply put young feet on the Old Trafford turf. He knows, as this book will elucidate, that the vast majority of youngsters he works with have no future in football. He knows he owes them as much care, if not more, than he does to those destined for the first team. He understands, also, that not all talent is equal, and that not every track is fast: for every Marcus Rashford, there might be ten Scott McTominays; for every Scott McTominay, there will be hundreds gone from the game long before the bright lights of the 'Theatre of Dreams' come into view.

'The ones that are going to be footballers, in the main, are right in front of you,' he says. 'You'd have to be blind not to see it. You'd have to be blind not to see the talent of Marcus

Rashford. Blind not to see the talent of Mason Greenwood. Blind not to see the talent of Ryan Giggs. Blind not to see the talent of Paul Scholes. Blind.

'For me, the art and the skill is finding those players who are actually under the radar and not right in front of your eyes. The majority of footballers are those players. The ones who come a bit later. They're not quite a superstar. A little bit like the Ugly Duckling – nobody really fancies them, nobody really sees them, then all of sudden the swan comes out. [McTominay] would be in that category. He was always a talented young kid and he was always going to be a good player, but I don't think anybody would have said he was going to play for Scotland or play in our first team at a young age. He's shown a lot of resilience, a lot of hard work, a lot of character. But there's others. They're scattered around.

'I'd like to think that I've been more than a football coach. I don't want to be defined as just a football coach. I want to be defined as someone who has wanted to help and support young people in life in general to get to where they want to get to, because in my experience it's not going to be professional football. Are we going to give up on the ones who aren't going to be footballers? I don't think so.'

The aim of this book is to examine how the latest generation of young English footballers – the likes of Rashford, Manchester City's Phil Foden and Trent Alexander-Arnold at Liverpool – have been developed, but also at what cost. The industrialisation of youth development has led to thousands of young people being swept into the academy system, yet opportunities at the highest professional level have never been in shorter supply. 'I think to be a professional footballer now is much harder than it was when I was a kid,' Whelan admits. 'I was competing against players from down the road, from Greater Manchester, possibly nationally. But now, you've got to be the best players in Europe. The stepping stones are much, much steeper.'

Through the stories and insight of those who power the academy machine – the coaches, directors, administrators and governing bodies, the players and their parents – *The Dream Factory* dives deep into this previously closed-off world. The curtain is pulled back to reveal the methods that produce the best players, but also how those deemed not good enough are discarded and what care, if any, they receive thereafter. Elite girls' academies are visited to chart the rapid growth of female youth development, and how it is approaching a decisive juncture the male game roared through – for better and worse – not so long ago. And the effect of money is laid bare by the juxtaposition of the wealthiest academies against those struggling to cover operating costs, how some clubs feel priced out by the rules that govern the system and how others aspire to thrive on meagre means.

This book aims to paint a rich, honest and comprehensive picture of football's academies, a system at once enriching and damaging to the young people entrusted to it; a world in constant evolution, where good people do great things and where the vulnerable can be forgotten; where the righteous and the profitable both reside but don't always play nicely.

'Youth development is an industry now,' Whelan says. 'I'm doing my best to keep up and try and stay ahead, but it's not easy.'

CHAPTER ONE

THE GREATER MANCHESTER DIVIDE

AS MARK LITHERLAND strolls the corridors of Bury's training ground in Carrington, Greater Manchester, the sound of dumbbells clinking against the ground, grunts of exertion and Stormzy blasting through the stereo system grows louder when he nears the gym.

A handful of the club's under-18s are putting themselves through extra work. They're striving to strengthen their sinuous, scrawny frames in the hope they'll soon be deemed ready and robust enough for the rigours of third-tier senior football.

'That's it. One more. Good!'

Man try say he's better than me. Tell my man shut up.

'Five . . . Six . . . Seven . . .'

Mention my name in your tweets. Oi rudeboy, shut up.

'How many is that now? I'll do one more set.'

How can you be better than me? Shut up.

Litherland walks with the confidence and contentment of a man at ease, at home. The forty-eight-year-old is in his sixth year as Bury's academy manager. In that time, operating under the stingiest of budgets, he has overseen the rise of twenty-five first-team debutants and generated almost £3million for the club's choked coffers through the sale of academy players.

He is proud of his work, proud of his staff, and rightly so.

Evidence of Bury's fiscal struggles are apparent from the moment you pull into the training ground's car park. The sprawling facility the first team and academy share, which used to belong to Manchester City, has fallen into disrepair. The prominent, light-blue facade is weathered, with the words 'ABU DHABI' and the outline of City's club crest still visible from where the previous signage was removed. The lettering replacing it is falling away: 'BURY FOOTBALL LU'. The lockers in the players' changing room were picked up second-hand from Liverpool's academy, a fitting metaphor for how Litherland's measly £5,000 yearly recruitment budget forces him to seek young players for the club. In winter, they uproot to a smaller, yet more modest facility in Bury, owing to an absence of floodlighting at their Carrington site. There is no girls' programme, nor a men's under-23s side, with a lack of financial viability the reason cited for both.

The club's fraught finances mean Litherland, day-to-day, faces a different kind of pressure to most academy managers. His responsibilities serve the club with vital cash flow, the first-team manager with a stream of good-enough youngsters, his staff with ensuring there is enough money left over to compensate their work fairly, and his players, their development and future careers.

But the weight he carries has not diminished his enthusiasm in the slightest.

As Litherland approaches the double-door entrance to the gym – a vast space, although modestly equipped, with cushioned matting lining the floor, free weights stacked neatly to one side and a row of black workout benches at the far end – seventeen-year-old centre-back Bobby Copping is on his way out. The tall, floppy-haired defender, whose youth is given away by the slight slope in his shoulders and the braces covering his smile, was signed from Norwich nine months earlier, in June 2018. He has already appeared for the first team.

'How many clubs were after you when we got you?' Litherland enquires.

'Thirteen,' says Copping. 'Stevenage, Bournemouth, Luton, Peterborough, Lincoln . . .'

'Why did you choose us?'

'Enjoyed it the most. Best potential to make it in the first team. I came here and went straight into the under-18s. Within three months, I made my first-team debut.'

Litherland's pride is evident – another success story. He pats Copping on the back and carries on making his rounds.

If you don't rate me, shame on you. If you don't rate me, shame on you.

In a little over five months, Litherland and all his staff would be out of a job, and all 140 of Bury's academy players, Copping included, would be released. In August 2019, Bury, who had been Football League members for 125 years and twice won the FA Cup, were expelled by the EFL amid spiralling, unsustainable debts. As of the time this book went to print, the club still exists, but – with no league membership, no players or staff – not in any meaningful way.

After a trial at Brighton, Copping resurfaced with Peterborough, signing a two-year professional deal with the League One side. In his first interview for his new club, the teenager heaped praise on the care and attention he'd received in his short but formative time with Bury.

'It was amazing,' he said. 'Mark Litherland and the coaches are unbelievable.

'It was like a real family.'

***

Manchester City work the ball up the pitch methodically, replicating the patterns of movement and precise, short passes they've practised thousands of times in training. The ball glides through midfield and forward, skidding across the turf like a skipping stone over a wide and serene lake. They send it left, meeting the advancing run of the winger, whose sharply angled cut-back from the byline finds the striker on the edge of the six-yard box. A side-footed shot is planted firmly between the posts, but it is blocked and cleared by the lunging sprawl of a desperate goalkeeper. No matter. The routine, nearly so successful here in the first minute of the cup final, will be replicated several times over, forging the game's opening goal as the seconds count down to half-time.

It's a sequence of play witnessed hundreds of times each season at the Etihad, City's home stadium which has seen trophies raised aloft regularly since the club was purchased by Sheikh Mansour bin Zayed Al-Nahyan and his Abu Dhabi United Group in 2008. The ownership group's investment in the club, as of accounts published in 2018, totals almost £1.5billion. They have comprehensively upgraded the training facilities, expanded the capacity of the stadium, invested in the best players and attracted the most revered coach in football, Pep Guardiola, to oversee the team's construction into an unstoppable juggernaut trained on unprecedented success.

On this mild evening late in April, though, as the sun dips behind the sweeping roof of the Etihad's Colin Bell stand and a pink and purple twilight illuminates east Manchester, the patterns of build-up play carefully designed by Guardiola are not being executed inside the 55,000-seat arena. Instead, 350 metres south-east, across the junction where Ashton New Road meets Alan Turing Way, it is seventeen-year-old Spanish winger Adrián Bernabé cutting the ball back from out wide, not Raheem Sterling or Riyad Mahrez; and it is eighteen-year-old Moroccan youth international Nabil Touaizi who scores to punctuate the sequence, not Sergio Agüero or Gabriel Jesus.

In their purpose-built, 7,000-capacity stadium, City's under-18s are hosting Liverpool in the 2019 FA Youth Cup final. The Academy Stadium forms part of the Etihad Campus, City's high-end, all-encompassing training facility. The impressive complex was built on eighty acres of former wasteland and derelict industrial sites at a cost of £200million and opened in 2014. The Etihad Campus contains within it the first team's state-of-the-art training area, injury-treatment and recuperation facilities, the club's office headquarters and the City Football Academy. The academy area alone – graded Category One under the Elite Player Performance Plan (EPPP) guidelines and in which more than 170 players, male and female, from the under-9s age group and up, receive world-class coaching – would put to shame the first-team training grounds of many a top-level club. Among its many luxuries, it boasts seventeen immaculate pitches, a 120-seat press-conference area and a hydrotherapy room. It is only ten miles from the Carrington site they bequeathed to Bury, but City's new base is a world apart.

The vast and fully equipped gym room houses on its main wall a mural of Agüero celebrating his famous goal against Queens Park Rangers, when the Argentinian's late strike clinched City's first Premier League title on the final day of the 2011-12 season. On one prominent wall of the main reception area is a quote from Mansour: 'We are building a structure for the future, not just a team of all-stars.' And a 150-metre pedestrian bridge extends between the Etihad and the Academy Stadium, aiding a steady flow of foot traffic between the two arenas and serving as a not-so-subtle metaphor for City's aspiring youngsters. The intention of City's heavy investment in their academy is clear: to create, in-house, stars of the calibre of Agüero or David Silva or Kevin De Bruyne, acquiring and nurturing the best young talent. It is all in the hope of replicating, for years to come, moments like Agüero's late winner against QPR in a more sustainable, cost-effective way – albeit with resources that dwarf the £5,000 Litherland was given each year to sign players for his academy and the one talent-spotter he employed.

That begins with indoctrinating the young players in the City way; the Guardiola way; in many respects, the Barcelona way. Many of the principles of Barcelona's famous *La Masia* youth system – which bred the likes of Lionel Messi, Xavi, Andrés Iniesta and Cesc Fàbregas – have been appropriated in Manchester by Guardiola, a former Barça player and manager, Ferran Soriano, City's CEO who used to be general manager of Barcelona, and City's sporting director, Txiki Begiristain, who formerly occupied the same role with the Catalan club.

'Everyone in the club is aware of the way we try to play, the way we try to progress the ball through the pitch,' says Gareth Taylor, City's under-18s manager between 2017 and 2020. 'All the managers and coaches will be on-board with our style of play. The manager [Guardiola] puts a big emphasis on that as well. The style of play, the process, to him is way more important than the result. If the processes are taken care of, the result will take care of itself.

'I certainly see Txiki a lot, observing academy games, under-18s games, Youth Cup games. He'll obviously have his priority, which is the first team, but he'll have a broader view on players, especially looking at individual players. He has a strong presence.

'We do a lot of problem-solving. We try and have an identity with the first team. I think this is the closest we've been to the first team in a long time [in terms of style] and that takes time to put in place. We have to make sure we follow the guidelines, that everyone understands the method and what our method is. The language is very important, the type of terminology you use. If you can get that into young players at ten, eleven, twelve, and also the technical components, that makes your job a lot easier by the time the players get to sixteen, seventeen, eighteen. We use a lot of Q-and-A in the auditorium. Out on the pitches as well, we try to extract information from the players, rather than this command all the time. I don't think that's exclusive to City; I think a lot of academies will be working in that manner.'

Against Liverpool in the Youth Cup final, City's 4-3-3 mirrors Guardiola's preferred tactical plan, as does their commitment to building from the back. Even when a mistimed pass from goalkeeper Louie Moulden presents Liverpool with a clear sight of goal, requiring impressive centre-back Taylor Harwood-Bellis to clear off the line, they remain undeterred from their high-risk, high-reward passing ethos.

The Youth Cup, running for close to seventy years, is the oldest and most prestigious youth tournament in English football. In the past, it has served as a springboard to stardom for George Best, Ryan Giggs and Manchester United's Class of '92, Michael Owen, Wayne Rooney and more. City have won the competition twice, but not yet since the 2008 takeover; they have reached the final in three of the last four seasons, beaten each time by Chelsea. Here, a goalkeeping error gifts Liverpool a second-half equaliser – a speculative twenty-five-yard strike from Bobby Duncan, a stocky, bustling striker who left City in acrimonious circumstances the previous summer, slips through Moulden's grasp. Liverpool go on to win a penalty shootout, with captain Paul Glatzel's decisive, confident strike into the top corner sending the travelling support into jubilant celebration in the Academy Stadium's west stand. It is a modicum of retribution for the defeat City's first team scored over Liverpool forty-eight hours earlier, with the two sides tussling over the Premier League title.

Another defeat at the last hurdle is a blow for City. The club no doubt crave success in the Youth Cup to signify their status as the best developers of young players in the country, with the best facilities, the best talent and the most attractive destination for future stars. Consolation comes from their triumph in the Premier League Cup, a title they would retain the following season, evidence of their standing among the elite of the English youth game. As Taylor consoles his players and ensures they stand and applaud as the trophy is presented, his disappointment is mitigated by the fact his boys played the better football on the night. They showed a clear identity in their play and, but for an unfortunate individual error, might easily have won.

Although he operated with humble means when compared with City in terms of both talent and budget, Litherland's work at Bury also drew heavily from continental influences in respect of the possession-based style of play he viewed as the best for developing young footballers.

Sitting in the video-analysis suite, a wide room adjacent to the office he shares with his most senior staff, where dozens of chairs face a blank projector screen, Litherland's admiration for the European game is evident. He begins to break down the tactical chess at play in the previous night's Champions League game, the second leg of a last-sixteen showdown between Juventus and Atletico Madrid. Fourteen hours have passed since the final whistle, but his brain is still abuzz with what he saw. He begins to scribble furiously, detailing how the Italian champions and Cristiano Ronaldo orchestrated a three-goal turnaround against Europe's meanest defence.

'Can I borrow your pen a second?' he asks, before bouncing out of his chair toward a nearby easel and blank sheet of A1 paper. 'How were this Italian, well-structured, well-defenced side going to get back in the game?' he asks, rhetorically. 'And how are they going to beat that 4-4-2, who are predominantly going to have ten men in their eighteen-yard box? And it was fascinating that they did it in the wide areas. It was unbelievable.

'If you look at it from a tactical point of view . . . I'll just go and get a marker.'

He rushes across the hall to his office and jogs back with a more suitable pen in hand.

'In these areas here, if you're getting a cross from here . . . You can go through them, you can go around them or over them – they went around . . . Then they had two big guys, who were Ronaldo and [Mario] Mandžukić . . .'

Litherland has a quarter of a century's coaching experience behind him, having moved into youth development when, at twenty-three, the discovery of an irregular heartbeat curtailed any hopes he had of a professional playing career. He joined Bury in 2014 and helped kick-start a profitable production line of young talent. 'Previous to me coming here, it had been eight years since they'd had anyone break through from the academy, so to do twenty-five in five years is just testament to all them really,' he says, sharing the credit with his colleagues and the players themselves.

Although the two are intrinsically linked, building for success on the pitch very much took a backseat to producing saleable players in the hierarchy of priorities to which Litherland worked. Rather than steering their best talent's development toward an eventual first-team debut, Litherland and his staff identified their highest-potential players early and moulded them with the requirements of higher-level clubs in mind.

'I'd say we're a little bit more patient in terms of releasing players,' Litherland says. 'We don't release that many players – at under-9s, -10s and -11s, we don't release players anyway, unless they fell out of love with it, or for personal reasons, family reasons. From under-12s up, that's when we start identifying, in terms of physicality, who's going to go on to make the next step.

'We do succession planning from under-11s up. That's identifying your best players in the age group. We do it in two: players who we think are going to get scholarships; and players of value who we think we're going to sell. For selling, they're outstanding, a bit special. It's been pretty accurate, if I'm honest with you.'

Litherland saw to it that Bury developed players in all positions who were comfortable and creative with the ball – particularly at centre-back, which became something of a speciality for the club – in an effort to both produce rounded footballers and attract the interest of wealthier clubs. 'We're a possession-based team,' he explains. 'Whoever we play against, whether it's under-9s through to under-18s, we want to dominate the ball. We played City last Monday with our under-14s. It finished 1-1. First half, they had the lion's share [of possession]; second half, we had the lion's share. How we see it is: you're not developing if you haven't got the ball, you're just running. We want to dominate the ball. In the league programme, from under-18s down, we constantly look to play out from the back.

'With that strategy, we've sold four centre-halves to what we call our customers, which are Premier League and Championship clubs. That's what they are looking for – ball-playing centre-halves who can play high up and defend one-v-one. We sold Jacob Bedeau to Aston Villa for £600,000; Emeka Obi to Liverpool for £300,000; Liam Williams to Sheffield Wednesday, £100,000; and Matty Foulds to Everton, £300,000.

'We're looking to try and develop thinkers rather than repeaters. You're making them think all the time. We might say to a group, "This is a problem. Now you go out and try and solve it." And once they learn how to do it, they've got it forever.

'I think a team going direct is neglect within under-18s down, because they're not developing with the ball, they're just watching the ball go over their head. In the first team, it's about three points. It's got to be a rounded education in the academy system – try and get the player on the ball as much as you can, all over the park. Then he'll develop his touch, his decision-making, his passing.'

Bury's location in City's former home was just a mile north of Manchester United's facility, which houses their Category One academy that has famously reared dozens of first-team stars, most recently the likes of Marcus Rashford, Mason Greenwood and Scott McTominay. City's state-of-the-art academy was just a twenty-minute drive away, too, and Liverpool, Stoke City, Blackburn Rovers and Everton all had Category One academies within an easily commutable distance.

For a low-budget, Category Three set-up like Bury's, then, competing for the best local talent was a futile endeavour. They did, however, look to capitalise on their locality when promising players slipped through the net at the bigger clubs nearby.

'We've got one recruitment guy,' Litherland laments. 'If you look at Man United and City, they've got seventy-five locally. We've got one. And, ultimately, we concentrate on the under-8s. We look to steal Man United's and Man City's under-8s, or Liverpool's. And we look to have the best possible twelve or ten players we can. That's sort of our foundation. Then we just add one or two bricks in between.

'If United release someone, are we aware of them? Normally, if they get released by a Category One, they want to stay in a Category One. They'll go to Blackburn, or they'll go to Stoke. To get them is difficult, but you can get them. How we got Sam [Allardyce, the former England manager's grandson] was Ryan [Kidd], who's the under-16s manager, knew his dad. There was a historical relationship.

'With Callum [Hume], when he got released by Man City, he went round all the houses, all the different football clubs. No one took him. We were basically the last resort. What you'll find with players who've been released by City is, they'll have an agent. I think one of the lads who's been released by City is on £70,000 a year now at Rangers. That's the level you're looking at.'

Despite their operating restrictions, Bury's relative success was impressive. Deep runs in the FA Youth Cup in each of the two previous seasons shone a light on the fine work done on the academy's training pitches, and four academy graduates made senior league debuts in the 2018-19 season. 'In the last two years of the Youth Cup, we finished fifth last year and we finished in the sixth round this year,' Litherland says. 'If you look at it in terms of budget, I spent £2,500 on recruitment last year. We are outperforming a lot.

'I think it's mentality. The staff have got a big-club mentality. If we go to City, we expect to win. We don't want to go there like a small club and surrender. We want to take them on. Ultimately, they train as much as us, so why can't we beat them? What you find is, then they want your players. Our under-10s won a big tournament at Man United. Man United, Stoke, Wolves – there were loads there, and we won. Our under-9s have won tournaments. We win a lot within the Foundation Phase.

'It's worked on average that we've made £500,000 a year for the football club, on top of what we get from the Football League. Ultimately, we've got to run as a business.'

The pathway between City's academy and first team has been particularly narrow in recent years. Prior to the 2020-21 season, the last academy product to make a sustained impact in City's senior side was former England defender Micah Richards in 2005. For all City's proclamations of wanting to see homegrown youngsters succeed at the club, their eye-watering investment in instant and ongoing first-team success is a competing interest.

Between the time he took charge in the summer of 2016 and the end of the 2018-19 season, Guardiola had given first-team debuts to eleven academy players. By May of 2020, those players had made a cumulative total of just forty-five Premier League appearances, with Phil Foden accounting for thirty-two of those. Four had left the club permanently and another three were out on loan. City ranked last among Premier League clubs for game time given to homegrown players in 2018-19; Foden was responsible for their entire total of 371 minutes of top-flight action given to academy graduates. Contrastingly, rivals United topped the table with 9,334 minutes played by academy graduates, with five homegrown players making fifteen or more Premier League appearances.

Taylor appreciates the challenges that have come with City's rapid evolution better than most. He initially began coaching with City in 2011, working on the club's Rishworth Project, an initiative privately funded by Mansour that gave a handful of Emirati teens the chance to experience life within City's academy. He then graduated into the role of under-16s manager, before being appointed under-18s boss in 2017. His association with City began much earlier, though, long predating the riches brought by the 2008 takeover. A Welsh international striker during a twenty-year playing career, Taylor spent two and a half seasons at the club's old Maine Road home, joining City after they'd been relegated to the third tier.

'I suppose for myself, and for anyone who played at City pre-2005, it's probably unrecognisable, the club at the moment,' Taylor accepts. 'And most of the supporters who've been around long enough would say the same thing. But I still think it's kept its culture, its personality. There have been huge, huge changes, and it's operating at a really high level at the moment. It's difficult to comprehend the difference from when I was playing [for City], from Christmas of '98 to the summer of 2001.'

The perceived lack of first-team opportunities for City's youngsters has seen them lose some outstanding prospects.

Jadon Sancho is, of course, the prime example, having turned down a contract reportedly worth £30,000 a week at City to join German side Borussia Dortmund in 2017. Only seventeen years old at the time, Sancho was a regular starter in the Bundesliga and the Champions League within six months of signing for Dortmund, and a first senior England cap arrived fourteen months after his move to Signal Iduna Park. City contest that, prior to his departure, a pathway to the first team was being cleared for Sancho; 'These are players that if you ask Pep today he will tell you they can and will be first-team players at Manchester City,' said City's chairman, Khaldoon Al-Mubarak, of Sancho and fellow academy standouts Foden and Brahim Diaz.

It cannot be known with any certainty whether Sancho would have broken through at City in a similar manner to his rise with Dortmund. But the winger, now coveted by the world's biggest clubs and valued at £100million, will feel content with his decision, having, by November 2019, played more than nine times as many minutes in the Bundesliga as Foden, just two months Sancho's junior, had in the Premier League. The other player cited by Al-Mubarak as a future first-team star, gifted Spain under-21 international midfielder Diaz, also slipped from City's grasp, leaving for Real Madrid in January 2019.

'In footballing terms, I wasn't a regular around the first team,' said Rabbi Matondo, formerly a promising winger within City's youth ranks, upon following Sancho's lead and signing for Bundesliga side Schalke 04 in 2019. 'I trained with the first team and it was a good experience training with Pep and the other players. They are top players. It is not City's fault; they have a wonderful team with wonderful players. But if you want to break in at City, it is not going to be easy.'

For City's academy investment to be deemed a truly successful enterprise, the bridge across to the Etihad needs to be more than an empty metaphor.

As a generator of revenue for the club, though, the academy is extremely successful. Although he won't be drawn on the specifics, Taylor admits the academy has targets it must hit for money raised through the sale of its young players. Such fiscal concern certainly isn't unique to City. The Premier League's EPPP manifesto, published in 2011, estimates that the cost of running a Category One academy is between £2.3million and £4.9million a year. Those figures have almost certainly increased in the time since. The need to sustain the cost of running an academy through player sales is a reality for most, if not all, clubs.

In May 2019, the *Daily Mail* estimated that City had made £125.8million in the previous five seasons through the sale of academy-bred players who had each made fewer than fifteen senior appearances for the club. Diaz's move to Madrid recouped an initial £15million, with a further £6.5million in conditional add-on fees potentially still to come; England under-21s goalkeeper Angus Gunn, who never played in a senior match for City, was sold to Southampton for £13.5million in 2018; and Schalke paid £11million for Matondo, who'd also never appeared for City's first team, in January 2019.

Most academy players aren't afforded the luxury of deciding to pursue lucrative alternatives the way Matondo and Diaz did, though; they are simply released, with no say in the decision to end their association with their club – a situation with which Taylor, who was released by Southampton at eighteen, empathises.

'It was the end of my world,' he says of finding out Southampton were to release him. 'I had no real formal qualifications behind me whatsoever. I moved from my digs in Southampton back to the West Country. I went on a number of trials – Brighton, Bristol City – but with no joy at all. Looking back on it now, they were also releasing their players, so I was really going to have to pull up some trees. I was still getting over the heartbreak of not getting through [at Southampton], because I honestly thought I was going to get a contract.'

Thanks to the endorsement of one of his former Southampton youth coaches, Taylor was given the chance to rebuild his career with Bristol Rovers in the third tier. He now feels a sense of personal responsibility for the players he's worked with who have fallen through the cracks, helping them find new opportunities as he had been helped at his lowest ebb.

'As an under-16s coach, it's a really tough role,' he says. 'You've got to be like a father figure to the players, you've got to try and instil discipline, you've got to prepare them for youth-team football. And then it's that aftercare of those who've been released. I probably have the best relationships with the ones who've left who I've kept in contact with. They might call and say, "I've been released from Newcastle," a club that you've helped to fix them up with, by having conversations with coaches, by having conversations with parents, giving your review of a player, and then helping them again – "Can you give me some advice?" Some of the lads who left, like Martin Samuelson, who left at eighteen and signed at West Ham, I kept in contact with. David Brooks was a lad I organised to go to Sheffield United because of the link I had there.

'It certainly helped me, that role, to develop my empathy. Having been in that position myself as a young player, being released, being turned down by places, it gave me a real insight into what was required to say to help. It was fortunate for me that I'd been through that process as well, had the ups and downs.

'It's the unforeseen stuff: the phone calls, the late-night ones, to check in with a player – "How's it gone?" when the player has gone out on trial somewhere. I think it's important. What helped me as well – and I'm not saying I'm perfect; I've made a lot of mistakes, a lot of errors – was having two lads of my own. I was doing the under-16s and I had a fifteen-year-old and an eleven-year-old. Now I've got a sixteen-year-old, and some of the lads in my under-18s are sixteen, so it's quite a nice barometer to use, especially the psychology of a young player, a young person – what's going on in the world, what's going on at school – all of those things.'

One of the players Taylor has worked most extensively with at City, and one in whom the club are confident of a long and impactful career at the Etihad, is Foden. A diehard City fan from nearby Stockport, Foden has been on the club's books since he was eight years old. While others, such as close friend and fellow former under-18s standout Sancho, have left for greener pastures, wider pathways, he has stayed. He trusted City to deliver on their word, that opportunities awaited him, that progress here might be slower than it would be elsewhere, but that, in the long run, it would be more rewarding. Taylor coached Foden for the best part of three years, first as under-16s manager, then in the under-18s. His experience working with the England international – who has come closer to meaningfully cracking Guardiola's first team than any other player to come under Taylor's tutelage – informed the approach Taylor took with his players.

'It's a great example to use Phil, in terms of being humble, being early to training and staying out afterwards,' Taylor says. 'Phil has always been top in that respect. Being a model pro, whether he's starting, a sub or not playing. He's a great example for a lot of the guys. Even for the sports scientists and the medical guys. When there's a programme players might not want to do, they can say, "Look, Phil Foden did this religiously, and now he can handle first-team sessions because of it." He's a great advert for us at the academy to use.

'I had Phil for nearly three years and I can't remember doing anything special with Phil. One of the things I did do with Phil was just be brave, play him in games where you think, "We're probably going to lose if we play him in midfield here because we're going to get trampled, but he needs to be in there." The easier thing to do would be to play him wide, on the wings, but then he isn't going to see the pictures you need him to see, because he had top scanning abilities even at that age. The main thing with Phil was backing him, being brave and putting him in there. If you don't do that, they're never going to develop the qualities you've seen glimpses of.

'And I think it's a balance. I think players learn a lot by not playing, as well. That's an important part of their progress. That sounds a bit contradicting, but, looking at some of the players who come through at under-16s and under-17s, they might not be a regular. There's not a set pathway for everyone.'

Foden became increasingly relied upon by Guardiola as a key first-team player following football's resumption after the coronavirus pandemic shutdown in mid-2020. By February of the following campaign, he had already matched his combined total for Premier League starts from the past three seasons.

As much as the coaches had pointed to Foden as a beacon, the embodiment of the commitment, patience and technical skill required of any young player with designs on a future at the Etihad, City's academy players will also have regarded the midfielder as something of a canary down the coal mine. If Foden – who, they were told, did all the right things and made all the right choices along the way – couldn't eventually achieve the ultimate goal of becoming one of the stars of Guardiola's side, those following in his wake would have felt they had little chance of doing so. Foden's breakthrough might save City from losing another Sancho.

***

Bury's 140 academy players had no choice but to find futures for themselves somewhere else in the summer of 2019. The close relationships Litherland had fostered with his young players only made it harder to break their hearts when the doors closed. He was never officially told that he was to lose his job as the club's collapse became apparent, was never thanked for his service or given any assistance by the club in folding the academy. But by the time Bury's expulsion from the Football League became national news, he'd long suspected the end was near. 'People's salaries started to come late,' he says. 'It just slowly deteriorated, month on month. The EFL gives you a £420,000 budget [to assist with the cost of running an academy]. We saw nothing of that money. As it got close to the time, we saw the writing on the wall.

'We brought our under-15s in on a day-release programme on a Thursday. I was out with them, doing some fitness work. It came up on Twitter then that the chairman had asked for a fundraising scheme on the day he needed to show finances. I think we all knew at that time that we were really in trouble.

'The lack of information, right up until the end, was disgusting. No one from the club told us anything. As it unfolded, we found out they'd been stealing our pension for four or five years. It just got worse and worse.'

Determined to do a more honourable, professional job of informing his players their future lay elsewhere, he gathered the under-16s and under-18s together at the training ground one last time.

'We tried to do it as professionally as we could,' he remembers. 'We sat them in a room and told them all.'

He then began to draft emails and make phone calls to the parents of each player in the younger age categories, imparting the same sad news. Most of the calls were greeted with tears, and fears about the young children's mental health, so devastated were they by the breakup of an environment that, in some cases, they'd been a part of for five years or longer.

'It took me a while to get over it,' Litherland admits of his personal struggle. 'My wife was great. She just left me alone for a couple of months.

'In the end, we raised the club around about £2.7million, with a budget of £5,000, which wasn't bad over six years. We would have raised a lot more, but some of the lads who went at the end, they went for peanuts. Bournemouth got Joe Adams for £50,000. Callum Hume went to Leicester City, and they were going to pay £600,000 but they got him for £50,000. It was scandalous really.'

Most of the players Bury released found new clubs. Litherland worked as a youth scout for Norwich City but was keen to return to the day-to-day hubbub of academy life. Bolton Wanderers later hired him to be their academy manager in August 2020. He was scarred by the way his work at Bury was so quickly undone, but he was not deterred.

'What doesn't kill you makes you stronger, at the end of the day,' Litherland says. 'I've learned from past experiences how to handle adversity, in terms of how to keep staff motivated when it's obvious they are going to lose their jobs. I feel that everybody was motivated, right to the very end.

'I see the players all wearing different-colour kits. I've got used to it now.'

CHAPTER TWO

GATEWAY TO A GOLDEN GENERATION

IN THE SHADOW of a grand manor house almost two centuries old and with chimneys and spires that rise three storeys high into the Shropshire twilight, fourteen-year-old Jamie Carragher was getting ready to run.

Lilleshall Hall was originally built as a hunting lodge for the Duke of Sutherland, and over time it has passed through the ownership of various members of the ruling class. In 1966, Sir Alf Ramsey's England team trained on the thirty-acre estate for two weeks before winning the World Cup on home soil that summer. A plaque commemorating the part the grounds played in that great triumph can be found on the wall of the house's Queens Hall bar, alongside a signed team photograph.

In the early 1980s, England manager Bobby Robson and the FA's then-technical director, Charles Hughes, formulated a plan to each year bring together the country's sixteen best fourteen-year-old footballers – to be whittled down from 2,000 contenders via a series of regional and national trials – and have them live, study and train together for two years. The plan was to create a pipeline of future England internationals by exposing the boys to uniform coaching practices in a controlled environment. Lilleshall, with its idyllic surroundings and handy location in the Midlands, was chosen to be the home of the FA's National School.

The programme ran for fifteen years, between 1984 and 1999, and produced more than a dozen senior England stars, from the likes of Michael Owen, Carragher and Sol Campbell to Alan Smith, Scott Parker and Jermain Defoe. (The standard of entry was so high that Steven Gerrard and Frank Lampard both failed to make it all the way through the selection process.) The selected boys left their parents and home lives to bunk in dormitories. The days were long and football-focused, rising early for breakfast and the minibus to school, then training into the evening and, on weekends, playing exhibition matches against the youth sides of local professional clubs. Most weekends also entailed a trip to a Premier League ground to study the professionals in action.

Discipline was high on the agenda for the young men bearing the crest of the Three Lions on their tracksuits. Every day, they were told, they were representing their country when they stepped out of the common room or sleeping quarters, be that in the breakfast hall alongside the menagerie of elite gymnasts and professional footballers recovering from injuries also on site, or at school or on trips to the shopping centre in nearby Telford.

That's why Carragher had to run. The indiscretion of the young Liverpool striker, as he was at the time, has long been forgotten. The memory of the punishment, however, is vivid. His target, precisely 1.6 miles from the main house, were the 'Golden Gates', exact replicas of the ones outside Buckingham Palace, which welcomed visitors into the grounds and on to the estate's long, winding driveway.

All the way there. All the way back. All by yourself.

'We used to call it the gate run,' Carragher remembers, 'when we'd get sent there and back if we misbehaved. If someone had done something or got into a bit of trouble, you had to do a gate run. You'd run it on your own; you couldn't run in groups. They'd set one off, and then they'd set another one off two minutes later, so you couldn't even talk to each other.'

'I had to do a couple, actually,' admits Danny Webber, the former Manchester United and Watford striker who, in 1998, was part of the National School's penultimate intake. 'We all had to do a few. Mr Pickering [the house master] would just drive along in his car. And I remember the FA was sponsored by Peugeot at the time, so he used to drive along in this maroon Peugeot and have his radio on while you're doing two miles there and two miles back.

'It was always the threat of a gate run – "If you do that, you're doing a gate run." As fourteen- or fifteen-year-old lads, you push it, don't you? Then you'd hear, "Right, get your trainers on," and your heart would sink. We did one at about half-nine at night one time. You just suck it up and carry on. It's character building.'

As daunting as it must have been for the boys to move away from home, and while homesickness certainly was an issue, most of the budding footballers were excited for the opportunity to be recognised as one of the nation's best and to test themselves daily against their peers. 'I think every football club sent the best two or three players in that year group,' Carragher recalls of the trial process. 'Myself, David Thompson and Jamie Cassidy were the lads who went to trials [from Liverpool]. I think it was a Sunday morning, at Preston's ground. It was a plastic pitch at Preston. We played sort of just games, really. From there, the three of us got chosen again then to go to Lilleshall. I think they had three trials at Lilleshall, and it kept getting whittled down.

'That was the first time I'd ever been to Lilleshall. We'd stay there for the weekend. You got to know lots of different people. Playing in the trials, you'd look at certain players who you thought, "He'll definitely get in." You can imagine that at that age – you're only thirteen, fourteen – everyone was talking, being at lunch together and sticking in your own groups. I think we had three trials at Lilleshall. And in each one, it just became smaller and smaller.'

Driving through the gates of the grand old estate for the first time might have been an intimidating prospect for a hopeful young boy, especially a working-class lad from Bootle, Merseyside. Carragher wasn't deterred by the unfamiliarity of these unusual, opulent surroundings, though. He was awed but inspired. 'It was like, "Wow,"' he says. 'You wanted to go. As soon as you drove into Lilleshall, you thought, "I want a bit of this. I want to be part of this." That big, long drive, you'd do it every day, to and from school, and it was spectacular. When you get to those gates and you drive in, it's almost like when you go into a famous football stadium, and you go, "Wow." That's what it was like at that age, going to Lilleshall for the first time. You just wanted to be part of it.'

'Obviously, we didn't have mobile phones back then, or pagers or anything,' Webber says, thinking back to the moment he learned he'd been selected. 'I used to go to the payphone at school every day and reverse the charges to call home and see if the letter had come. I did that for about three weeks – "Has the letter come? Has the letter come?"

'Then, one day, the letter had come, and I said, "Just open it." I'd been accepted. It was in lesson time at high school, so I couldn't tell anybody. I went into the toilets and looked in the mirror. I had a little buzz to myself that I'd managed to get in.'

The Lilleshall boys attended Idsall School in Shifnal, a small market town of around 6,000 inhabitants a fifteen-minute drive away. They'd be ferried there and back every day, with special dispensation to skip lessons on Tuesday mornings and Friday afternoons to cram in extra training; any missed school work had to be made up in the evening. Long before the academy system was formalised, and before the introduction of the Elite Player Performance Plan locked in a club's educational commitment to its young players, the schooling arrangements seen at Lilleshall set the template for what would become common practice in later decades.

Despite the efforts made to normalise the school routine of the Lilleshall boys, integration wasn't easy. The local youth didn't always take kindly to the allowances made for the arriving football stars, nor the attention they attracted. 'We felt like outsiders,' Carragher says. 'We were all given the same coat, which didn't help – thirty-two lads get off a bus every morning with the same Umbro coat. We stood out a mile. And you can imagine lads in the school not being too fond of these superstar footballers coming from all over the country to go to their school. And you can imagine what the girls were like, with footballers from all over the country. Some of the lads were going out with the girls.

'There'd be trouble now and again. There'd be the odd fight. The football coach, Keith Blunt, was really good: "If one of the lads is in a fight, you're all in a fight. You back him up" – that type of thing, whereas the housemaster was a bit like, "Don't get involved."'

'There was always tension, from day one,' adds Webber, who'd swapped inner-city Manchester for the leafy Shropshire countryside. 'I had a couple of fights. It was one of them where you have to mark your territory a little bit. It wasn't easy for the local lads, because you've got sixteen lads who have come into the school, who have all got a bit of something about them. And it's a novelty for the girls. You get a bit of attention, but jealousy from the lads. It causes a bit of friction. It's something you have to deal with.

'We used to go to the cinema on a Friday night. That was our only little time out. We'd get the coach to Telford, where we were allowed to go to the cinema. That was the only couple of hours where you were allowed out of Lilleshall but you weren't in school. Again, you would meet girls or whatever it may be. Inevitably, local lads would come down and want to cause trouble as well. You have to back yourself a little bit. There was always a bit of friction.'

But the wall-to-wall football on offer at Lilleshall, the players felt, made up for any social speed bumps they encountered.

'It was total football,' enthuses John Curtis, the former Manchester United and Blackburn defender who joined the National School the year after Carragher. 'It was: get up in the morning, sometimes train before school; sometimes we'd go to school, come straight off the bus and get changed, go and train. You were living as an apprentice professional while doing your GCSEs, basically. All the players loved the game, loved playing the game – that's where they felt most comfortable. Every time we played, we'd play in England shirts, and we'd play against local academy teams. It was a great experience, fantastic.'

One player who did encounter some football friction was Joe Cole. A supremely skilled midfielder signed to schoolboy forms with West Ham at the time, Cole was part of the same intake as Webber. Diminutive but blessed with an exquisite first touch, the vision to carve open any defence and the imagination to dream up and execute moves most players would never consider, the teenage future World Cup star struggled initially with the conservative, one-size-fits-all nature of the coaching. Ever the entertainer, Cole performed a Cruyff turn in the centre of the pitch during one training session and quickly found his exuberance had drawn Blunt's ire – 'We won't be having any of that nonsense here, lad,' yelled the gruff Yorkshireman.

'Joe was probably the best talent that England had seen for a number of years,' Webber says. 'He played off the cuff. He played with immense street talent. If you put him on a pitch, he could do anything. I always remember, in the first few weeks of training, Joe was not enjoying himself as much as he should be. The coach was telling him to pass it where he wanted to dribble. He was like, "I don't like it. They're trying to tell me to pass all the time. I want to beat people. I want to dribble."

'We came back after the first weekend home – we'd go home for a weekend once a month – and fifteen lads came back. Joe didn't come back. We were like, "Where's Joe? Why hasn't Joe come back?" And we realised that Harry Redknapp, who had him at West Ham, said he's not coming back. He'd gone back to West Ham for the weekend, enjoyed himself, and said, "Look, I don't want to go back. They're trying to coach the dribbling out of me." Harry had said he's not coming back, and he ended up having a conversation with the FA to basically say, "If you're going to knock all this natural talent out of the boy then he's not coming back." A few days later, they'd come to some agreement, and Joe came back with all the freedom in the world.'

More content upon his return, Cole eventually thrived, and he now ranks as one of the National School's most prestigious alumni. The strict rules and disciplinary measures the players were subject to could leave the boys feeling a million miles from home at times, with some from early intakes labelling the main house the 'posh prison'. And no promises of future prosperity were made to the gifted kids – 'The fact is,' Blunt told 1993's inductees, 'only two of you here will probably go on to make it as a top-level professional footballer.'

But despite the gate runs, the social awkwardness and the inevitable homesickness, almost without exception the players selected to stay at Lilleshall reflect positively on their two years at the former hunting lodge. Most still treasure the commemorative cap presented to them by a legend of the game – former England international Jimmy Armfield one year, Jimmy Hill another – in a graduation ceremony at the end of their stay. Disciplinary leeway was granted at the right times, too. Although he'd initially been banned from his graduation proceedings after getting into a scuffle at school, no one stopped Carragher taking part and collecting his cap. In those two formative years away from home, skills were honed, careers were launched and lifelong friendships were founded.

'I loved it,' Carragher affirms. 'Absolutely loved it. The best players in the country would train against each other every day. It can only improve you as a player. I can't say whether it meant I "made it" and went on to do what I went on to do, but it played a big part in it.

'It was a great experience, when I look back on it now. I would rather do that at Lilleshall than have played Sunday-league football, which you were still allowed to do back then. It was nowhere near the standard I was playing then, coming up against Marlon Broomes and Ronnie Wallwork in training, who were the two best centre-backs in the country at that age and I was a centre-forward. It was a great grounding and I loved it.

'We got together twelve months ago. They all came up to Liverpool and we had a night out, twenty-five years since we left Lilleshall. We're all on a group chat now. We're all still heavily in touch with each other.

'I really enjoyed it. We still have a WhatsApp group with all our lads on it now,' Webber says. 'We meet when we can. We go and have a beer or we meet up and have a day out somewhere. We've created memories and friends for life.

'From a footballing point of view, it pushed me out of my comfort zone a lot. You're not always the best player on the day. There are other players that are of equal, if not better, ability. It pushes you. I think the discipline and the structure around the schoolwork was important as well. It taught me a lot of lessons, not just as a player but as a person. I think it was a very good thing.'

The FA's National School programme was ended in 1999 off the back of the *Charter for Quality*, a nationwide review of youth football which former Leeds United manager Howard Wilkinson was commissioned to produce. The Lilleshall project had long been a point of contention for many clubs. They resented having to allow players they'd signed to attend without being given oversight of the coaching methodology. Many perceived the centralised school to be slanted too far in favour of producing players for the national team, rather than for their parent clubs. Wilkinson recommended that the National School close, and that clubs be empowered to replicate a similar model themselves.

'I think it's a shame that it stopped,' argues Curtis, who now holds a prominent position within the United States Soccer Federation as a coaching coordinator, 'because I think with hindsight and knowledge, they could make a better job of it now.'

In the end, Lilleshall's legacy lies not only by the England stars it birthed but also by its influence over how the modern academy system was shaped in its image after the Golden Gates closed.

*** *** ***

Professional football clubs have operated youth-development programmes, in some form or another, for almost a century. Manchester United are credited with formalising the first affiliated youth policy. Responding to fan pressure from supporters in the 1930s to include more local players in the team, chairman James Gibson and club secretary Walter Crickmer started the Manchester United Junior Athletic Club as a means of attracting the region's best talent.

While, over time, other clubs followed suit, the English Schools FA (ESFA) remained the predominant power in English youth football for much of the rest of the century. Professional clubs were not allowed to sign young players to any kind of formal contract until they were fourteen, when associated schoolboy terms could be offered. As such, although boys – and later girls – could train informally with a famous club, the bulk of their football would have been played at school, as well as with grassroots Sunday teams after local and county leagues were developed in the 1950s.

In the 1980s, in the face of repeated failure at senior international level, the FA drew criticism for its perceived lax attitude to developing young players for the professional game and was encouraged to take a more active developmental role. In response, the National School at Lilleshall was opened in 1982. However, this programme catered only to the elite few selected to attend. For the vast majority, the structure remained the same: schools and Sunday football and informal training with professional clubs until at least fourteen years of age.

In January 1997, just four months after he'd been sacked as Leeds United manager, the FA hired Howard Wilkinson as technical director, instructing him to get right to work on a comprehensive review of the English youth-football system. The document he produced, entitled *A Charter for Quality*, would initiate the most seismic changes youth football in England had ever known, plotting the blueprint for the modern academy.

Then in his mid-fifties, Wilkinson had amassed a wealth of experience in the game, dating back to a playing career which began in the early 1960s, through to twenty years in management, including a largely successful eight-year spell with Leeds. Although he was best known for guiding the Yorkshire club to the final First Division title before the English top flight transformed into the Premier League in 1992, it was Wilkinson's unseen work at Leeds that best prepared him for the reshuffle of youth football he was about to oversee.

'At Leeds, in '94, I got the new training ground, built accommodation, and then formed a partnership with the secondary modern down the road, so that our youngsters could go to school, like at the National School,' Wilkinson explains. 'We could have a session before school, we could have a session after school if we wanted. And it worked at Leeds, because by the time they played in the European Cup semi-final, well, that's the stat that I quote: when I got to Leeds they'd signed eighteen [sixteen-year-olds to apprenticeship deals], and only one was a professional at the end of it; towards the end of my time at Leeds, I think we signed seven in the penultimate year, and six of them were on the sheet for the European Cup semi-final [in 2001], the [Jonathan] Woodgates and so on.'

Wilkinson studied the methods employed by successful youth systems abroad, such as Ajax and Barcelona, and contrasted those with what he found back home. The comparison, as far as the English practices were concerned, was not favourable. He found that the English youngsters were playing a dangerous number of games – up to 100 each year, between club, school and county commitments – and that they were not being exposed to proper technical coaching early enough. All the other clubs he studied took their players on board younger than was the case in England, with Ajax providing three weekly sessions for players as young as eight, and even Sao Paulo in Brazil coaching kids from twelve. Fewer games and more structured sessions, that was a lesson also gleaned from Lilleshall, where an example of achievable optimum 'contact time' was set.

'It was cruelty, overplay,' Wilkinson says. 'And they were playing, but playing is not necessarily learning. Competition still prevailed, in the sense that people wanted to win the league or whatever. It was counterproductive in terms of developing players. And one of the aims was to produce better players that might play for England and have a better England team.'

The National School also served as a template for the way Wilkinson envisaged the children's education being integrated with their football development, in much the same way he had initiated at Leeds. In English football, the Youth Training Scheme (YTS) was introduced in the early 1980s, with, supposedly, the players who don't go on to a professional career in the game provided the cushion of vocational training or academic study alongside their football. The boys signed to YTS forms upon finishing school at sixteen would complete menial tasks around the club – cleaning senior players' boots and mopping changing rooms – as well as undertaking, for example, a course in leisure management or general studies. The educational offering of the YTS programme largely failed to engage its young footballers, though, and clubs tended to show little interest in ensuring the academic side of the agreement was taken seriously. When Wilkinson devised his plan for a new academy system, with clubs bound to providing recognised and worthwhile further-education options for their players, he found the different nomenclature of the old and future ways of operating to be illustrative.

'I suppose one could sum up the difference, pre-academy and post-academy: pre-academy, they were called apprentices; and post-*Charter for Quality*, they were called scholars,' he says. 'I think those two words give you an idea of the difference. Very different connotations.

'What you want for [the players] was that they get the best opportunity to be the best whatever it is, and person as well, that they can be. I mean, that's just the most basic thing you hope for. Even if you say you're a maths teacher, and my kid is at your school and he's in the maths group, don't think I'm going to be happy because you can turn him into Einstein but he's a prick.'

To some surprise, Wilkinson recommended the closure of the National School at Lilleshall. He instead insisted that the onus for developing the next generation of the country's footballers be handed to the professional clubs. Five years on from its formation, the Premier League was already a financial juggernaut, the collective spending power of its clubs far outstripping that of the FA. The *Charter for Quality* outlined a new academy system, whereby clubs who applied for a full academy licence – initially recommended to be all Premier League clubs, but dozens of others wanted to follow suit – were told they must run teams from the under-9s age group all the way up to under-21. Those who wished only to operate a less-intensive centre of excellence were required to provide teams from under-14s. This meant the prominence of schools football would shrink, with the best players now asked to prioritise playing for their clubs. The extent to which the ESFA was subsequently diminished was laid bare when the FA purchased the rights to the England Schoolboys under-15s team from them for £1.5million.

Staffing levels were increased under the *Charter* and long-overdue child protection measures were put in place, one of them being a rule against clubs recruiting players from farther afield than a ninety-minute drive from their academy campus. It was stipulated that academies must hire heads of education, and the subsequent influx into the game of teaching professionals not only added much-needed expertise on the educational side but also brought credible child-protection experience. A plan was drawn up to construct a new FA centre in Burton on Trent, too, where coaches could be developed. That ambition, though, frustratingly for Wilkinson, was not fully realised until St George's Park was opened some fifteen years later.

The changes laid out by the *Charter for Quality* were wholesale and sweeping. The level of investment it sought to inject into youth football was unprecedented. And with real change, inevitably, comes resistance.

'For us to make that change,' Wilkinson explains, 'the *Charter* had to be ratified by the FA. That means it had to go through a full FA council meeting, of which there are 103 councillors, and they represent all factions of the game. I think it'd be fair to say that there were quite a few who were against the *Charter*, but for all sorts of reasons.

'Football clubs thought it was taking away some of their freedom to operate anywhere they wanted to operate. For instance, before the *Charter*, Newcastle could sign a boy from Portsmouth on a schoolboy form age fourteen. And then between fourteen and leaving school, never see him again but have his registration in case when he was sixteen he had become a better player. Travel distances were reduced. You'd got people travelling miles and miles for a session.

'During my first year and a quarter there, I had probably over 200 meetings, trying to convince people of the benefits. We convinced them and we got the vote through to the FA after twelve months – 101 for, one abstention, one against, I think. But right at the beginning, there were only about six or seven who said, "Yes, we'd like to become an academy." And then, as is the way in life, once six or seven became academies, others thought, "What are we missing?" So that quickly jumped up to double figures.

'You'd have to be an idiot not to look at it and see that this offered you a much better opportunity to develop players.'

Over the next decade and a half, several efforts were made to refresh and rejuvenate the youth-football model the *Charter for Quality* created. The most notable of which was an FA-commissioned report by Richard Lewis, the chairman of Rugby Football League. Published in 2007, Lewis's *A Review of Young Player Development in Professional Football* made sixty-four recommendations for systemic improvements. But elite youth football in England remained largely as Wilkinson had envisaged it until the advent of the Elite Player Performance Plan in 2012, a reimagining of the game's youth-development structures more controversial even than the *Charter* had been fifteen years previously.

Representatives of just six Premier League clubs – including Manchester United, Arsenal and Chelsea – came together to draft EPPP. Implementation of the plan would see a greater education provision (some clubs cover private school fees in excess of £10,000 per year for each player signed to a scholarship contract), to which players continue to receive access even if they are released before the natural end of their studies. Facilities would be further upgraded, child-protection measures made more robust with the mandated appointment of a safeguarding officer at every club. Each academy would be measured against a set of criteria around facility, staffing and coaching levels and assigned a status of Category One (for the best), Two, Three or Four. Independent audits would be completed regularly, with ambitious lower-ranking academies allowed to apply for higher status should they match the requisite criteria.

With the Premier League on board, EPPP was rolled out to the seventy-two English Football League clubs, although the vote on whether to adopt the new proposals was far from unanimous – forty-six clubs voted in favour, twenty-two against, with one abstention and three no-shows.

The ratification of EPPP meant standards of coaching, education and facilities within elite-level academies was at an all-time high. And the Premier League's Elite Coach Apprenticeship Scheme (ECAS) quickly accomplished what it took the FA more than a decade to achieve with St George's Park, providing opportunities for coaches to pursue their own development, with obvious trickle-down benefits for players. When EPPP was first introduced, there were 250 coaches employed full time by academies in England; there are now more than 800.

EPPP has unquestionably made the youth-football world an altogether more professional environment, and its architects will, not without reason, claim it is a big factor in the development of the current generation of gifted young English players. But the reason EPPP has not been embraced with universal open arms is twofold.

Firstly, there is the cost factor. The 117-page EPPP document, first published in 2011, outlines the expected yearly costs associated with running an academy at each Category level. A Category One academy is said to cost between £2.3million and £4.9million, with a Category Two topping out at £1.8million and a Category Three at £540,000. While funding of up to one third of the total cost is provided to offset this outlay, the figures in the initial EPPP document are almost certainly now outdated. It is believed the typical cost of running a Category Two academy is now around £2.5million annually, for example; some relatively modest Category One programmes run on an annual budget of £5million, and the bigger-spending academies are believed to be eating up a yearly budget of £10million or more.

Upon the introduction of EPPP ahead of the 2012-13 season, Hereford United, Wycombe Wanderers and Yeovil Town all decided these were costs they couldn't justify and so closed their respective youth systems. Brentford decided to fold their Category Two academy in 2016, opting instead for a B-team model of recruiting only a few young players of genuine first-team potential and, in the process, they claim, saving themselves £1.5million a year. Huddersfield Town and Birmingham City have since followed suit. Bolton Wanderers, who once operated a Category One academy, have downgraded all the way to Category Four, unable to sustain the spending required for the higher grades in the face of financial difficulties.

The second key factor contributing to the unpopularity of EPPP, especially among smaller clubs, is how its prescribed player-valuation system is perceived to favour those with the biggest budgets. Under EPPP, every player who completes a season in a professional club's academy, from the age of nine and up, is assigned a value. The size of the figure attached to a youngster's registration correlates with how many years they have spent in their club's system and at which level the academy in question is graded. For a player in the Foundation Phase (under-9s to under-11s), their assigned value is £3,000 for each completed year. In the Youth Development Phase (under-12s to under-14s), it ranges from £12,500 per year for a Category Three academy to £25,000 per year for Category Two and £40,000 per year for Category One. If a player joined a Category One academy at under-9s and stayed right through until under-16s, they'd be 'worth' £286,000. An additional £150,000 can then be tacked on for every ten first-team appearances up to sixty games, and then a further £100,000 for every ten games up to 100.

Much aside from the sheer unseemliness of placing a price tag on the head of a nine-year-old, this system can, in theory, lead to players becoming trapped when they want to leave a club but can't find a new team willing or able to meet their stipulated compensation fee. A 2017 BBC report found that clubs waive the compensation figure in more than eighty per cent of cases when players wish to leave, but the potential for impasse is rife.

This is not the main root of the clubs' objection to the compensation system, though. While it was designed to ensure that smaller sides receive a fee for players poached by the bigger teams, many clubs feel the prescribed fees don't accurately reflect the value of their best players, and that Category One academies – who, under EPPP, are no longer bound by the ninety-minute travel radius and can recruit nationally for players aged fourteen and up – find these figures eminently affordable as they hoover up and stockpile the top talent. The loss of strikers Ian Carlo Poveda and Joshua Bohui to Manchester City and Manchester United, respectively, was the final straw for Brentford, who claim they received only around £30,000 for each player.

'Category One status can trip some clubs up because suddenly it's like kids in a candy shop: "I'll have one of them and one of them,"' Ged Roddy, the Premier League's former director of football development who oversaw the implementation of EPPP, admitted in a 2017 interview for *The Guardian*. 'The most productive clubs tend to use their environment more and recruit principally from around their locality, maybe integrating one or two others after that. There's a lot to be said for putting some restrictions on yourself, even if you're not required to by the rules and regulations.'

Leaving it up to the wealthiest few clubs to gird their greed and self-regulate their drive to acquire talent en masse is certainly a novel idea. Unsurprisingly, not everyone is buying Roddy's line.

'It's probably the biggest issue for our clubs,' says David Wetherall, the EFL's director of youth development. 'It certainly was when the Elite Player Performance Plan was brought in. Fixed compensation, our clubs were generally not in favour of it, and I think if there was a vote now, I don't think that view would have changed. But it is what we have in place at the moment. It's part of the system and we'll see how it develops over the coming months and years.'

'I think there's no rhyme or reason to it,' Colin Gordon, who until recently was chairman of Kidderminster Harriers, says of EPPP. Although Kidderminster, sitting outside the Football League, are not under the auspices of EPPP, Gordon has spent most of his post-playing career as a coach and agent to up-and-coming young players, so he has seen the churn of the machine up close.

'The whole organisation is driven by the elite few,' he continues. 'No one wants to upset them. No one wants to put checks and balances in place. Everybody wants to blame everybody else. There's no leadership at all in EPPP. They think that they're putting some regulation in, but all that regulation does is give people who don't want regulation an opportunity to circumvent the regulation. So that's all that happens.'

Gary Issott, Crystal Palace's academy manager, is slightly more circumspect but no less insightful in his appraisal of the regulations. 'I think youth development needed modernising,' he says. 'The benefits [of EPPP] are I think it's improved facilities, improved environments, improved staffing levels for young players, improved contact time. But it's created a little bit more player movement than you'd like. I think that's the unhealthy aspect of it.

'Losing your best player at fourteen for £250,000, or at sixteen for £400,000 – and this is Category Two – it's not great. It doesn't protect the clubs well enough. And it also incentivises the buying club to take a gamble, whereby they're not really serious about a player. If you're serious about a player and you're putting up excellent money, there's a commitment there that you've got to try your best to develop them, rather than buying four or five lower-tier players and hope that one comes through. That's not fair on the players. It shouldn't be allowed where clubs can stockpile players.

'You can recruit nationally at fourteen. The issue with that is, if we were to find a boy in the north-east or the Midlands, you've then got to move him and his family down, or you potentially take him away from his family at fourteen. How many success stories have there been of that? I think [Jadon] Sancho left Watford at fourteen. I think that's what the EPPP needs to look at and quantify: how many players has that been good for? Even at sixteen, that's a challenge. You're moving a family. If it does go wrong, you've taken somebody who, for example, has their roots in the north-east, to London.'

For all the good that EPPP has ushered in – the elevated standards across the board and the players produced – there has unquestionably been a cost, human and financial. The compensation model and the ability of the wealthiest academies to free themselves from the ninety-minute catchment rule when recruiting has exacerbated the disparity between the upper and lower links of football's food chain, accelerating the market for talented young players into dangerous overdrive speeds. When Manchester United and others first founded affiliate youth clubs, they were designed to be refineries for the best local talent and a means of reaffirming a cherished connection to their place and their people. In that sense, the modern academy machine is in danger of losing touch with its humble beginnings.

CHAPTER THREE

DOORSTEP DIAMOND MINE

'SOUTH LONDON AND PROUD' reads the hoarding that borders the carefully manicured pitches of Crystal Palace's academy. Past the old gatekeeper's cottage, across the cobbled car park and up into a pavilion building overlooking six full-size pitches, Palace's youngsters come and go. On the field at the foot of the pavilion's concrete steps, under-23s coach Richard Shaw is running his team through a series of fast-paced *rondo* drills. The pap-pap-pap of the ball resonates, a percussive accompaniment to the bustle above.

Academy manager Gary Issott sits inside, where a lunch buffet of chicken and rice and vegetables and pasta is to be served imminently, and where the bar area and weathered burgundy carpet gives the feel of an old working-men's club. Soon, the sound of studs click-clacking up the steps will signal the end of Shaw's session, and lunchtime for players and staff. The quiet bar room will become a thronging concentration of talk and clinking cutlery. Coaches will discuss plans and appraise progress. Teenagers will bat banter back and forth. Laughs will billow. For now, Issott sits in still contemplation, reflecting on his academy's most recent success story of almost exactly a year earlier: the rise of Aaron Wan-Bissaka.

'He didn't let anyone down,' Issott says of the baptism of fire that saw a twenty-year-old Wan-Bissaka start against Tottenham in his debut, with games against Manchester United and Chelsea following, all within the space of thirteen days. 'He had to mark [Christian] Eriksen, [Alexis] Sánchez and [Eden] Hazard. He earned the trust of his manager.'

Wan-Bissaka's emergence in February 2018 is the most significant first-team breakthrough propelled by the work of Palace's academy in recent years, even if luck played a major role. The full-back was under consideration to be loaned out to a Championship team before a spate of injuries to first-choice defenders left manager Roy Hodgson with little choice but to turn to the homegrown hopeful for a series of key fixtures against some of the Premier League's toughest opponents.

Palace lost each of the three games by a single goal, but Wan-Bissaka impressed sufficiently to nail down a starting berth for the remainder of the season, even earning the club's Player of the Month award for March. The following season saw him take Player of the Month honours three more times before being anointed Palace's Player of the Year. Just sixteen months separated his unheralded first-team arrival and a move to Manchester United which made him one of the costliest British players of all time.

The key to the Croydon-born defender's preparedness for his fortuitous first-team opportunity lay in the fact he'd faced such make-or-break moments before. Signed as an eleven-year-old after being scouted playing for local grassroots side Junior Elite, there was debate among Palace's academy staff over whether to release Wan-Bissaka, who was playing as a winger at the time, at fourteen. Within a year, he had kicked on and developed into one of the club's standout attacking talents. And it was by chance that Wan-Bissaka later came to play in defence. One Thursday morning during the 2015-16 season, he was among a group of under-23s players making up the numbers for an eleven-v-eleven drill in first-team training when he was asked to fill in at right-back. This put him in direct opposition to Wilfried Zaha, one of the Premier League's most feared and skilful wide men.

'I remember it really well,' says Kevin Keen, who was a first-team coach with Palace at the time. 'The manager asked for some of the under-23s to come over, and they didn't have a right-back. I said, "Just bring Aaron over and I'll play him at right-back." So Aaron came over, played right-back against Wilfried Zaha, and I thought, "Hold on a minute, this boy knows what he's doing as a right-back", because Wilf is very hard to defend against. I made a note of it mentally, and then the next day I did the same. The following day he played against Andros Townsend. Again, he did really, really well and showed a fantastic defensive mentality. That raw material was there to be seen: his strength, his power, his understanding about how to defend against two top-class international players. It was very natural. All of a sudden you think, "This boy could be a top Premier League defender." So I spoke to Richard Shaw. I said, "For the next few games, play Aaron at right-back and see how he goes."'

It is part of Issott's staff's job to ensure that, as far as is possible, their young players are ready to make the most of such opportunities. Exposure to the senior side will not always come under favourable circumstances for academy players, so a certain comfort in unfamiliar positions is fostered early. 'We try and give them a mixture of positions younger down,' Issott says. 'Then at eighteen, nineteen, it's a finishing school: if you're a right-back, here's all the finer details of being a right-back. There's so much to learn.

'It's the same with the systems we play. By the time they go on loan and someone asks them to play a diamond, they need to know how; if someone asks them to play 3-5-2, it can't be the first time they've been asked to do that, because that means we haven't given them the right education. The style of play [mirrors the first team]. But within that identity you still play different systems and apply different tactics for the players' education.'

In a 2016 article, *The Guardian* detailed how fourteen per cent of the English players in the Premier League at the time hailed from within a ten-square-mile patch of south London, with Croydon, where Palace are based, bordering one corner and Orpington, Woolwich and Lambeth the other three. The borough of Croydon alone was said to have produced five per cent of all English Premier League players, including Zaha and Wan-Bissaka.

In 2020, Palace completed the requisite upgrades to their academy facilities and infrastructure to apply for Category One status under the EPPP guidelines. The award of the higher licence enables them to cast their recruitment net nationwide. When graded at Category Two level, their recruitment of players aged under sixteen was restricted to a catchment area with a radius stretching an hour-and-a-half's driving time outwards from the academy site. They were free to target players aged sixteen or over from anywhere in the country, but, almost without exception, the best talents have long since been snapped up by that stage. Being situated in such a rich talent hotbed, Issott feels, has been both a gift and a curse. 'Because of our Category Two status, it's almost ninety-nine per cent [local recruitment],' he says. 'We're allowed to recruit nationally at sixteen, but by that time a lot of the best players have gone. We've taken foreign boys in recent times, but ninety-nine per cent is from south London.

'If you're in a one-club city, you've almost got the pick of the players first. Of course, we've got a good catchment area, well populated. But we've got fourteen professional clubs in London. With EPPP, everyone's recruiting better – the rules have dictated that – and it's fierce. The north-west, they've got eighteen clubs up there. Us and the north-west, where it's very well populated, there's nothing like it. And we've got three Champions League clubs – Chelsea, Arsenal and Tottenham.'

Despite the local competition for talent, Palace have held their own over the last decade, producing a number of players who've broken through to the first team and gone on to command hefty transfer fees when sold elsewhere. The sales of Zaha and Wan-Bissaka alone, who were both sold to Manchester United, with the former later returning to Palace, have recouped around £60million for the club.

For Issott, the greatest thrill his role provides is the fulfilment of seeing an academy prospect make their debut for the senior side. He still remembers the first debutant he oversaw – seventeen-year-old defender Lee Hills coming off the bench in a 2-0 defeat to Watford at Selhurst Park – and he glazes over reminiscing about Victor Moses's ascent and the potential the winger possessed. 'Ultimately,' he says, 'you are desperate for your young players to play at your club because supporters love it, owners love it. Everybody can connect. If a lad from South Norwood or Brixton goes and plays in our first team, someone will know him that went to school with him. It just unites everybody. You need it.'

Issott was, by his own admission, 'an average midfield player' during a brief playing career that encompassed a couple of years as a professional with Luton and six months in the United States, 'just through desperation to still be called a professional footballer'. He began coaching at twenty-two and spent four years within Tottenham's academy, as well as working with the FA to develop coaches and serving as Stevenage Borough's under-19s manager. He's been at Palace since 2004, when he joined the club as under-18s boss. Despite being only in his early forties, he has amassed a wealth of coaching experience which he calls upon in helping shape the raw materials Palace mine from the local talent pool.

One of the biggest challenges of Issott's role is not one unique to him or indeed football, but one faced by anyone working with large groups of young people from a variety of backgrounds. More than most academies, though, Palace's location and catchment area sees them draw from a broad range of cultures. For instance, lunchtime brings together under-18s striker Will Donkin – an Oxford-born, Eton-educated Chinese Taipei international signed from Chelsea – and under-23s defender Ryan Inniss, who hails from nearby Penge and, through the drug dependency and imprisonment of his parents, had to take a lead role in raising two younger siblings as a teenager. Inniss has had several off-field troubles, including a 2015 conviction for assault. Managing, safeguarding and encouraging young people from diverse and disparate backgrounds requires a careful and empathetic approach from coaches and management alike.

'For me, personally, coming from leafy Bedfordshire to here at twenty-seven, it took me eighteen months to two years to skillset myself to deal with all these different issues,' Issott admits. 'I had to really educate myself and understand that there's a reason for every behaviour and trace it back to where that behaviour was learned, tap into the players' mindsets.

'Team spirit is fine but it's managing individuals, keeping individuals on a straight line and not allowing them to self-destruct. And understanding why some days they might come in and they might be low, because not all of them have got perfect backgrounds in London. Some of our players live below the poverty line in the schoolboy age groups. I remember one player was consistently late. My first instinct is to punish the player. When you trace it back, he was coming from a cultural community where the children do the jobs in the house, and his dad wasn't allowing him to leave the house until he'd completed all his tasks after school. You experience all these things. It makes you broader and wiser and more empathetic. Rather than one size fits all, you've got to be bigger than that.'

Though they might arrive from vastly different backgrounds and home lives, once through the academy doors, every player's goal is the same: to eventually break into the first team. To that end, there is a line of messaging that hits home universally: the example of those who've been there and done it, the stories of the likes of Zaha and Wan-Bissaka and their paths through the academy and across Copers Cope Road to the adjacent first-team training ground. The example of Zaha is one Issott and his staff find especially useful as a motivational aid, because, despite the Ivory Coast winger's immense natural talent, he didn't stand out as a prospect of particular note for some time.

'All the time, you're making reference to him with the schoolboys,' Issott says. 'And you're just storytelling. At fourteen, I couldn't tell you what he was going to become. Was he in the top ten? Yes, but he still had so much to do. At seventeen, he got in the team, then it was like, "Wow." You can try and comfort players. There's only a very small amount who think they're good enough. You can say, "Wilf would have had the same thoughts as you. Aaron would have had the same thoughts as you. They've all been in your shoes. I can tell you now, they weren't the best players, but every day . . ." And the constant message is: work hard. Concentrate.'

Palace's plans for the academy's expansion were unveiled in 2019, with the development costing £20million. As well as an all-weather dome and bespoke classroom facility, a new medical centre is included, plus revamped canteen space and meeting rooms, all of which are shared with the club's girls' academy, which runs independently of the boys' side Issott oversees. Palace currently employ thirty-five full-time and 100 part-time academy staff, and they expect that number to increase by approximately twenty post-upgrade. Although Category One status allows them to sooner cast wide their scouting net, Palace harbour no illusions about being able to compete for the best talent with the likes of Manchester City, Chelsea and Liverpool on a national scale. Their doorstep hotspot remains their bread and butter, with, they hope, their improved facilities a greater lure to lock down the best local talent. 'Securing Category One status for our academy is imperative for us to be competitive in attracting the very best young players, and there is an abundance of raw footballing talent in south London,' said chairman Steve Parish, prior to the club's plans being given the green light by the Bromley council in November 2019.

No matter how many high-potential youngsters Palace are able to attract, and no matter how rich a seam south London is to mine, the brutal reality of elite youth football is that opportunities for advancement to the first team, and for long, prosperous careers in the game, will always be in short supply. Running boys' teams in ten age groups between under-9s and under-23s, Palace have as many as 200 academy players on their books at any one time. Yet in the 2018-19 season, Zaha and Wan-Bissaka were the only academy graduates to start a Premier League game for the club, with the latter becoming Palace's first academy player to make a full league debut in almost six years. For many young boys in south London's poorer communities – one in five children in Croydon live below the poverty line – Zaha and Wan-Bissaka are beacons guiding a route out of hardship, a path that runs directly through Palace's academy. These success stories will be myths for the majority, but Issott's hope is that every player who passes through Palace can reflect positively on their journey, irrespective of the ultimate destination.

'If you've been at a professional club,' he argues, 'you've learned some key disciplines, you've had some great experiences. You should've become a better player through it, which then gives you the ability to earn some side money through it in non-league. You've seen parts of the country that you wouldn't have seen as well.

'I think it's sad that a lot of clubs don't have local boys, because although we talk about the heartbreak [of not making it], the experience should be enriching.'

***

Craig Liddle lives a hectic working existence. Middlesbrough's academy manager is often seen briskly pacing the long hallways of the club's training ground, pulled between one meeting and another. There might be parents to placate, loans to organise, development plans to discuss. Now, though, he has found five minutes of respite. He sits in his long, rectangular office, reclined in a chair in front of a desk next to the room's only window. Beneath a windowsill lined with trophies, a plaque commemorating a 2015 UEFA Youth League meeting with Torino rests on a small table, alongside a magnum of champagne, a red, leather-bound copy of the Holy Bible and a spray can of bug repellent. Whiteboards adorn the walls, inked with training schedules and players' development plans. A low blue sofa is weathered and worn from the steady stream of visitors to his office. It is a room as busy as Liddle's average day.

Written in red pen on another whiteboard above the sofa is the club's stated values: 'To pursue success and sporting glory on the field and be a flagship for and positive influence on the community.'

Middlesbrough's commitment to their local community is more than just a virtuous slogan to be memorised by staff and players. Driven by the club's long-time chairman, local businessman Steve Gibson, Boro have a sincere desire to represent and support the town of Middlesbrough and its people. This ethos is imbued into every level of their academy, and the clarity of that vision connects the dots between every disparate duty under Liddle's cluttered remit.

'First and foremost, we want to get the best talent from within our area,' Liddle says. 'Within Teesside and Durham, we want to get the best talent that's around. We've obviously got competitors in Newcastle and Sunderland. It is tough. It gets tougher now, because people start to recruit at younger ages. We actively want to look at the area and the surrounding areas. But I'm not naïve enough to think that you're going to compete unless you broaden the regions you're going to look at. We do look nationally and internationally to top up on the local boys that we've got, but, first and foremost, we want to get the best local boys.'

While there isn't the same congestion of elite football clubs in the north-east of England as there is in London or the north-west, Middlesbrough's two main local rivals, Newcastle United and Sunderland, also operate Category One academies. In a part of the world where football passions run deep and are dyed in the wool at birth, deeply entrenched loyalties and fierce competition for talent can make Boro's chosen recruitment strategy a slog. But Liddle, a former Middlesbrough player who first began coaching the club's young players in 2000, feels this local focus brings more benefits than downsides.

'The area just oozes football,' he says. 'Everybody knows about it, everybody wants to talk about it. No matter where you go, if people know you're involved in football, they want to talk about it. It's a very passionate area, and that's something I don't see changing.

'Football is a way of life up here. I've lived up here most of my life. All my friends are season-ticket holders at Newcastle, so I was brought up as a Newcastle supporter in my younger years. Football is bred into you at an early age. People do take an interest in the younger age groups. Everybody wants to pull on that shirt for Middlesbrough on a Saturday afternoon when they grow up.'

The north-east isn't considered as rich a talent hotpot as Crystal Palace's location in south London, but Middlesbrough's faith in local youngsters is reaping dividends. Nine academy graduates – including Liddle's son, Ben – featured in the Championship for Jonathan Woodgate's first team in the 2019-20 season. According to the website TrainingGroundGuru.com's 2016-17 Academy Productivity Rankings – for which each professional academy in the country is ranked according to the number of graduates playing senior football in the top four divisions – Boro have the ninth-most-productive youth system in England, ahead of rivals Newcastle and Sunderland and even Manchester City.

'When you look at the mission statement from the chairman, it's to give people from the local area an opportunity,' says Peter Hood, Middlesbrough's assistant academy manager, speaking two days before their under-18s, with Steve Gibson in attendance, will lose narrowly to Manchester City in the 2019 Premier League Cup final. 'That's not to say we won't recruit from other areas. We will, and probably more so in the last couple of years. Recruitment is changing. It'll change again with Brexit. Our success, predominantly, over the last fifteen, twenty years – we always have success with local talent.

'You go to our games and you hear them sing "Stewie Downing, he's one of our own." There's a genuine, genuine pride from the fans when a player comes through.'

Key to Middlesbrough's ability to maintain an upper hand in local recruitment are the six development centres they operate throughout the region. Many clubs utilise similar satellite schools – for example, Chelsea operate eleven development centres around London and the south-east. This, Hood believes, further strengthens Middlesbrough's community connection and helps them spot the best youngsters as early as possible, keeping their production line bountiful.

'Generally, by twelve, thirteen, fourteen, the best players in the area are connected to clubs,' Hood explains. 'That's where your recruitment is key. Local recruitment, eyes on the ground, is key to what we achieve. If you see a little diamond at nine, ten years of age, they'll be brought in here to train. It's important that the community is at the forefront.'

Scott Sellars, the head of academy at Wolverhampton Wanderers, shares Hood's belief that a football club, and especially its academy, should plant its roots deep within its community. 'I feel that the academy is seen as a vital part of the football club,' Sellars says. 'Morgan [Gibbs-White, the first-team midfielder] is a Stafford boy from just up the road. Niall Ennis is a local boy. Ryan Giles, who played this year, is from Telford. I think fans definitely have a pride in seeing local players coming through. And from our point of view, the football club, the owners see it as an investment. They don't want to be spending £30-35million on a goalkeeper every year. They want to be spending maybe £1million for you to produce one.'

Sellars has been with Wolves since 2014 and was made academy boss in early 2019. When he arrived in Wolverhampton, the club had only recently been promoted back into the Championship after dropping down to the third tier. Since then, the Midlands club have been acquired by Chinese conglomerate Fosun Limited and pumped with funds to transform them into Europa League contenders. Sellars experienced similar sweeping changes in his previous role, as Manchester City's head of academy coaching from 2009 to 2014. He is keen to ensure a pathway to the first team is better protected for Wolves' youngsters than he experienced at City, allowing academy hopefuls and young fans alike to be inspired by the likes of Gibbs-White.

'Morgan at sixteen was in the under-23s,' he says. 'He came as a scholar and we put him straight in the under-23s because we thought that was his appropriate challenge, that would make him elite, that would push him on quicker and that would maximise his potential.

'I think there's nothing better than being in an environment where somebody is there and you can go, "I want to be like him." That was the difference at City, because people would go, "Why am I coming in? I'm never going to get there." I think here's different. We're very lucky that Nuno [Espírito Santo, Wolves' manager] has a first-team squad of seventeen outfield players, so every day, three, four, five under-23s players train with the first team. He doesn't want a big squad, so the opportunity is there. If they get injuries or suspensions, the next players in the first team are the under-23s. He can't go and sign anyone else.'

Wolves' Chinese owners have spared no expense in crafting a senior team capable of competing for major honours, but the academy is not being fiscally indulged in the same way. In addition to balancing the opportunities provided for local prospects with the recent influx of continental – particularly Portuguese, owing to the club's relationship with super-agent Jorge Mendes – imports into the club's youth set-up, Sellars has been tasked with making the academy a self-sustaining enterprise. His remit has become a delicate balancing act of generating funds through player sales and making sure Nuno's thin squad is sufficiently supported. But he is determined that success won't come at the cost of community.

'I would hate to think that if we closed the academy down, there's a young boy from Wolverhampton that will never play for the first team because he has to go somewhere else,' he says. 'That's the big negative. I would love to think that Wolverhampton fans' sons want to come to play for this academy.'

CHAPTER FOUR

THE TALENT ARMS RACE

'THE NUMBER SEVEN who played in that team, is he your son?' asked Rob Winzar. The Chelsea scout had just witnessed a six-year-old Mason Mount play his first-ever game of competitive football on a grass pitch. Smaller than most of his peers, Mount was drowned beneath the baggy, yellow-and-black, Borussia Dortmund-style shirt of grassroots side Boarhunt FC, but his skill, determination and aggression in pursuit of the ball grabbed Winzar's gaze. Familiar with the boy's father, Tony, from the local non-league football scene, the scout enquired about having Mount attend a training session at Chelsea's Cobham academy the following Friday.

Tony Mount had spent sixteen years as a manager in the lower divisions, taking in spells in charge of Havant Town and Newport Isle of Wight. Although he knew little about the inner workings of an elite youth academy, he had worked with several players who'd been discarded by top-end talent factories. He saw no reason to rush his son into such a cut-throat environment.

'Look, he's only just started playing on grass and he's very young – he's six years of age,' he told Winzar.

'Well, we take them from that age,' countered the Chelsea scout. 'We take them into our academy, then there's a process they go through. We look at them, and if they're good enough, they go into an elite squad, and from there they go into the academy.'

'I just want him to enjoy his football and let's see where it takes him,' Mount Snr said, cutting short the conversation. 'Thank you very much, but I don't think we'll be there on Friday.'

They would be there soon enough, though. Employing a wily trick of the scouting trade, Winzar invited the entire Boarhunt squad to Cobham three weeks later for a 'football festival', a weekend tournament that, thanks to Mount's star turn, Boarhunt would win. Despite the reluctance of the player's parents to have their son enter an academy environment at such a young age, the tournament invite meant Chelsea's scouts and coaching staff could assess Mount at close quarters, and the boy could be beguiled by the setting.

'Once we've got them in at Cobham, it opens their eyes up,' says Winzar, who still considers the six-year-old Mount to be the most exciting prospect he's laid eyes on in more than fifteen years talent spotting for Chelsea. 'That was what did it.'

'I knew what was going on,' Tony Mount remembers, reflecting on the period when his son, now a regular starter for Chelsea and England, first began to attract attention from professional clubs. 'They invited Boarhunt to what they called a festival. The chairman of Boarhunt, Kev Neil, phoned me and said, "I'm just letting all the parents know . . ." He was buzzing over it. "We've got a great little team. We going there to this festival, it'll be a great day and the boys will love it." I'm like, "Yeah, OK."

'From four years of age to six years of age he'd been playing indoor football at a place called Soccer City, which was all about fun and enjoying it, and he loved it. One of the parents asked me if he'd get involved with Boarhunt, and I thought, "Let's get him on grass. Let's see if he takes to it on a freezing-cold Sunday morning." And to be approached and be given a sales pitch about an academy, it was a bit of a shock and out of the blue.

'It's a tournament. You go along. It's the first time you've seen what the facilities are like at Cobham, and the boys are there. They're one of about forty teams playing in a mini-soccer tournament. There are lots of people there walking around with Chelsea tracksuits on. Every time the boys were playing, there were people watching. I knew what was going on. They were looking at the boys and assessing. That's what they do, I presumed at that time. At the end of the festival, which Boarhunt won, Mason came over to me and his mum and said, "They want us to come over Friday night. They've invited four of us up to train. Can I come? I want to come. Is it OK?" And so it begins.

'We brought him up to the development centre. It was a Friday night. Some of the boys from the festival were there, I recognised some of them. It was like a training session, but it was great fun, and Mason loved it. The quality was good, the standard was good, the coaches were good. At the end of it, Mason was like, "They want me to come back next Friday. Can I come back Friday, Dad?" Little did I know, that would be happening for the next twelve years.'

The Professional Football Scouts Association has a published list of dos and don'ts advising its members on what is considered proper conduct when on duty trying to spot the next great talent for their employers. Nothing about Winzar's work-around for getting Mount to Cobham contravenes these ethical guidelines, and both Mount and his father reflect glowingly on the player's journey through Chelsea's academy, from the moment he arrived on the premises as a six-year-old; this is evidenced by the fact that, despite also training regularly with Portsmouth – the club he supported – and Southampton, Mount chose to commit to Chelsea when the time came to sign exclusively with one club at under-9s level.

That other such high-profile clubs were also in the hunt for Mount illustrates just how competitive the youth-scouting world has become. And the player's ultimate decision to sign with Chelsea shows the value in a club presenting themselves as the earliest and most ardent suitor.

'You have to move fast if you've seen something,' says Stephen Wright, the former Liverpool defender who now scouts for the club in North Wales and Chester. 'You know for a fact there are other clubs there, not just you. Sometimes you speak to the coaches and say, "Can I have the parents' number?" They can then prep them, and say, "Listen, a Liverpool scout was here today. And there was a Man United and a Man City one." And then it comes down to, is the kid a Liverpool fan? Is he a Man United fan? These are the things you have to deal with as well.'

Identifying talent and analysing potential is only half of the job. A scout must also be a skilled salesperson. Working for a club like Liverpool, a player at the level Wright aims to uncover will almost certainly be on the radar of competitors. His mission, then, is to extol the virtues of his club, convincing player and parents alike that there is really only one destination worth considering.

'If a kid is there and he's willing to come, you've got to sell him the club,' he says. 'If they want to ask things, you've got to be one of the right people to ask questions of. If you're trying to sell the club to players, you only have to look at Trent [Alexander-Arnold]. There is a pathway. If there's not a pathway, parents do ask the questions – "You've not had a kid through for a long time . . ." They're right. It's there in black and white, the stats and data all show it. And then when you've got the kids playing in the FA Cup, like we had, that's even better. Jürgen Klopp, the manager, is very vocal in saying, "I haven't got a problem with those players playing." He's very meticulous in the way he works and he loves youth. If you're good enough, he'll give you an opportunity.'

Scouts are a club's eyes and ears on the ground, the first point of contact with a world of potential waiting to be tapped. They are the straw through which their club's increasing thirst for large volumes of talent can be sated. Whether within or without the fine margins of what the trade itself considers ethical, this responsibility to feed the academy machine, to be first and most convincing, can lead to unscrupulous behaviour.

'Scouts have been known to give parents their card in the car park and stuff like that, but to me that's unprofessional, unethical,' says Martin Taylor, a former scouting coordinator for Chelsea and Arsenal. 'It gives your club a bad name, gives you a bad name. Once you get a bad name in football, it sticks. Whenever I went to a game, I would always inform the managers I was there. You don't want managers to think you're there, hiding behind a tree or something like that. Most managers like that. They like the approach, professional. If I liked a player, I would ask the manager if I could speak to the parents. I would never go straight to a parent. That is the best way to go.

'I remember once being at a game, there was a scout standing behind a tree. It was pouring with rain, and all you could see was the umbrella sticking out the other side of the tree. You knew he was a scout. It was obvious.

'I was a bit naughty when I was a lot younger,' Taylor admits. 'I managed to get into Arsenal [as a Chelsea scout] one Saturday afternoon, and watched their under-8s, -9s and -10s all playing matches. I got found out on the way out, though. I actually stood with a parent. It was raining that day and I stood under their umbrella so nobody could see me. I wouldn't do that now. That was when I was very young, green and naïve. I think a scout should act professionally at all times. You're the first person a manager or parent sees from that club. You want them to have a good reaction towards you.'

Taylor also recalls how bending the rules to attend a tournament where scouts were prohibited led to one of his proudest discoveries, that of Rhian Brewster, whom he signed for Chelsea. 'I went to a tournament in Woodford – I think it was at Woodford school,' Taylor begins. 'I went in, and I met a guy there called Dan Seymour. He was running a team called Shield Academy; he was the manager. It said no scouts on the day. I was talking to Dan, and I said, "I've got to go out." He said, "No, come and be my coach for the day with Shield." He gave me a Shield top. I put that on. There was a scout there from Arsenal, who I'm good friends with now. I went to the people in the tent and told them there's an Arsenal scout there. They threw him out. I was the only scout in there.'

Much like Mount when he was spotted by Winzar, seven-year-old Brewster was playing his first competitive football matches at the tournament. And like Mount, he was small for his age, his baggy, red-and-white-striped Shield shirt billowing in the late-summer breeze, and he stood out for reasons beyond his sheer speed and skill.

After dribbling half the length of the downsized pitch, beating two defenders and lashing the ball into the top corner of the shrunken goal, Taylor realised the kid was someone he needed to watch closely. The scout found what he considered confirmation of the boy's extraordinary potential shortly after. When Brewster was felled by the sliding tackle of a bigger opponent, he rose quickly to his feet, dusted himself off and winked at Taylor, his stand-in assistant coach for the afternoon. Moments later, when the same opponent was carrying the ball downfield, Brewster crashed in with a firm sliding challenge of his own. He stood up. Dusted himself down once more. And winked at Taylor.

'I just knew then he was a player,' Taylor says. 'He had that character, he had the desire, he had the technique, the agility.'

As soon as the games had finished, Taylor introduced himself to the player's mother, who had accompanied her son to the tournament, and invited the boy to a Chelsea training session. He was then put on the phone to Brewster's father, who was 260 miles north, in County Durham, watching a Test match between England and the West Indies at Chester-le-Street.

'Look, I just want him to enjoy football with his friends,' was Ian Brewster's initial, reticent reply. 'I don't want him to be off at this academy. He's so young.'

***

Ian Brewster was eventually persuaded to allow his son to train with Chelsea upon learning that the boy, at least until his under-9s season, wouldn't be bound to the club. He'd still be free to play for Shield, for his school team and recreationally with his friends.

As was the case with Mount and Brewster, though, being prohibited from signing them to a binding contract doesn't prevent clubs from attempting to stockpile and sift through as many children as young as five and six as they wish. While some clubs will run sessions for a small group of players aged six and up at their main academy base, many use development centres to assess these youngsters in hordes. These satellite training bases are often located far from the academy site, enabling the club to expand their catchment area beyond the ninety-minute-drive radius to which their academy is bound, tapping into talent pools farther afield. They can also cycle through a greater number of players, holding open trials or sessions for larger groups, potentially scrutinising the abilities of hundreds of kids each year, selecting the best for more formal coaching and, eventually, a place in the academy proper at eight years of age.

This was the case with Brewster, who attended Chelsea's development centre in Redbridge, east London, one of eleven such satellite schemes the club operates. The player's father remembers being struck by the sheer number of boys who would pass through the development centre, and the seeming disposability of those who don't make the grade.

'They've got these satellite classes all over,' Ian Brewster says. 'They pick the best out of every one, and they make up the elite group that trains at Cobham. Rhian only had about three or four sessions at the satellite centre and they whipped him straight into the advanced group.

'What they do, they just filter them through. You'd be talking to a parent one week, then you don't see them again. They'd be filtering them out. I think eighteen boys they whittled it down to. When I spoke to a scout, he said, "You don't realise how lucky you are, because Rhian has come in right at the end and he's got straight in." He said to me, "Roughly, we'd have gone through 350 to 400 boys."'

Manchester City have been known to run sessions for children even younger than the age at which Brewster and Mount were scouted and snapped up by Chelsea. In 2019, City received criticism when a team photo depicting their 'Under 5 Junior Academy Elite' group, as the image's caption described it, circulated online. These four- and five-year-olds, pictured proudly in full City kits, met three times a week to train at the club's luxurious academy. City will almost certainly not be alone in providing formal coaching for players so young, but the backlash they incurred centred around the perception of their having imposed a degree of professionalism on these barely-school-age kids, kitting them out in club gear and labelling them 'elite'. On average, just one in every 200 eight-year-olds in a professional club's academy goes on to make even a single first-team appearance, and, as such, critics felt it was reckless of

City to bestow false hope upon these children and single them out among their peers.

'The reality is that they will probably be released by the age of nine,' Nick Levett, the head of talent and performance at UK Coaching, told the website TrainingGroundGuru.com. 'There's the issue of identity foreclosure, in which the child has an identity without having explored other options or ideas. When that's shattered there can be wellbeing issues. At the age of ten or eleven they are in a better place to cope with that, but not at four. Don't take a photo like the first team. Don't call it elite. There are also the kids who haven't been selected for the elite squad. To be told you are not good enough at four, when you can't eat your tea without spilling some, is just not common sense. The worry is it becomes common practice.'

City declined to comment on the matter, but, according to TrainingGroundGuru.com's report, an insider at the club claimed the picture and the furore it sparked 'misrepresents what really goes on at that age level', and that the sessions are 'fun', that the children are 'not registered with the club' and that they 'often play for other clubs as well'. Even so, such protestations do little to address many of Levett's concerns.

Part of the theory behind the drive to expose children to high-level coaching at ever-younger ages is that they are believed to have a greater capacity for learning new motor skills between the ages of six and twelve, the so-called 'golden age of learning'. It is thought that such early repetition and refinement of football's fundamental techniques and skills will better ingrain them within a player; the official age-group teams within Barcelona's famed academy, for example, begin at six years old. To extend this line of thinking, then: every year a gifted young footballer does not receive regular structured coaching from the age of six, they might later end up playing catch-up – or, worse still, in the eyes of the clubs with a vested interest in their future, already be marginally reducing their true potential. This is why, after studying the methodologies of successful youth systems abroad, the FA's *Charter for Quality* in 1997 reduced the age at which clubs could sign players, from the under-14s level to under-9s, and allowed for an increased training schedule.

But there is a delicate balance to be struck between developing the best possible players and allowing kids to be kids. Many key figures within high-end academies in England are sensitive to this issue and would like to see the age at which players can be formally signed to be raised, yet the arms race for talent continues to grow fiercer. Fully capitalising on the 'golden age' is just one factor behind the strive to attract the best players younger and younger. The desire to acquire and stockpile talent is a greater, more sinister driver. It is cheaper to rear a superstar in-house, even accounting for the hundreds of players discarded in the process, than it is to buy one on the transfer market. And hoovering up as much of the talent pool as possible, at as young an age as possible, means there is less left for rivals.

In 2020, Bayern Munich took the admirable step of deciding to no longer sign players younger than twelve to their academy. Even though a large number of coaches and academy managers would like to see a similar approach adopted in England, it is unlikely to materialise without the imposition of regulation. Bayern occupy a privileged position at the top of the food chain in German football. Much of their success over the past decade has been built on their cannibalisation of the Bundesliga. They can feel comfortable about their decision to allow the rest of the country's clubs to fight over the best talents younger than twelve, safe in the knowledge that, at a later stage, their financial might and historical standing will allow them to cherry-pick from their competitors anyway.

A similar move in England would rely upon an agreement being struck between the handful of the country's most powerful clubs. The prisoner's dilemma strand of game theory explains why this is unlikely to happen. The theory dictates that two or more individuals might not cooperate, even if it is in the best interests of all to do so, for fear one party will renege for their own benefit and to the detriment of the others. This is the dynamic at play in English football that prevents its top clubs from following Bayern's lead: while they all might agree that recruiting only from the age of twelve and up is desirable, if there are no strict rules to enforce it, one club refusing to comply would stand to scoop the best young players. And so the arms race perpetuates.

Even those on the front line of the scramble for wholesale talent, the scouts, would be in favour of a change of tack. 'I would stop scouting players from under the age of ten,' admits Martin Taylor. 'I would start academies at under-11. What I've seen in the past is players of six, seven, eight blown up out of all proportion – "He's going to be the best player. He's going to be a world-beater." They're not at the club when they're twelve, even ten. I think a kid should be developed naturally and nurtured.'

One parent of a high-profile young international player, who preferred not to speak on the record or be named, railed against what they perceive as football's culture of 'child trafficking', and how clubs' stockpiling of talent damages the individual's development.

The competition for the best young players has seen parents wooed and sold the football dream in order to secure the services of their offspring, too. Just as the pre-teen players can become enamoured with the idea of wearing the official kit and training gear of a top club, so too can their parents be charmed by strolling the halls of the club's training ground or being introduced to the first-team manager. And the charm offensive only ramps up as the player progresses. By the time they turn fourteen, a particularly gifted player can find themselves the object of desire for any and every Category One academy in the country, whose recruitment is no longer restricted to an area within a radius of a ninety-minute drive.

'Word on the street was getting out that Rhian might be available,' Ian Brewster remembers of the summer his then-fourteen-year-old son's two-year registration period with Chelsea was set to expire. 'That's when my phone started ringing. All of a sudden, people I didn't even know were ringing me.

'How did they get my number? I do not know. I had Man United ring me. He said, "We always knew Rhian was a good player; we've watched him. However, we never thought we'd get a chance to get him, hence why we haven't ever contacted you. We understand now there's a possibility maybe. Would you mind coming down to have a look?" I never went. Man City as well, they wanted to see us. Never went there as well.

'We went to one club, spoke to them. The bloke put his arm around me and said, "You know, this is only the beginning if Rhian comes here. There'll be a lot more where this has come from." We got looked after. We got invited somewhere and treated like royalty. It wasn't about that. It was all about Rhian, getting him the platform to show his skills. For me, that's what it's about.'

Brewster decided to leave Chelsea that summer and sign for Liverpool, enjoying five years with the Anfield club, even collecting a Champions League winners' medal, before joining Sheffield United for £23.5million in 2020. But the player's father is quick to insist the move to Liverpool was entirely the teenager's decision, and that the family were most impressed by the developmental plan the Merseyside club presented to them. The attempts of the other interested clubs to curry favour with Brewster's parents, in the end, only drove them away. Other families in their position might not have been so clear-sighted.

Although Mason Mount elected to shun all offers in favour of staying at Chelsea and forging a future at Stamford Bridge, his father recalls a similar experience to Brewster's dad at the same stage, with two of the Premier League's biggest clubs fighting to lure his son away from Chelsea at fourteen.

'Mason's not stupid,' Tony Mount says. 'At fourteen, fifteen, he'd looked at the same boys I'd looked at. He'd watched people like Jacob Mellis, Sam Hutchinson, Jack Cork, Gökhan Töre, Fabio Borini, Jérémie Boga. He's watching all these boys coming through and not playing and looking to go and leave. The door wasn't open. There was no pathway. Mason was as aware of it as me. Although his heart was set on Chelsea, I felt, as his dad, I had to give him other options if they were there, and they were there.

'We had a number of clubs [make their interest known], but there were two that really stood out – big clubs, on the same level as Chelsea. We went and met them and I was very impressed. They had videos on him, stats on him. They did reports, knew his strengths and weaknesses. They summed him up. They'd done their homework. They wanted to relocate him, put him in a private school and give him a pathway.'

Tony Mount only reports positively of the conduct demonstrated by the two clubs he met, and that he sensed no underhanded efforts at inducement such as those Ian Brewster detailed. His experience with agents, however, opened his eyes to how some parents are coaxed into cashing in on their son's football talent.

'Mason was playing for England youth,' he remembers. 'We were in France. I went to a bar with my wife and a couple of friends. Two guys approached us and basically offered me £200,000 to have Mason on their books.'

His response to the offer was to laugh. He believed that, somewhere down the line, there would likely be a quid pro quo for which his son would be liable, despite the agents' insistence that the sum would be a gift in return for the right to represent Mason.

The offer was given short shrift, but it is easy to imagine how a family less financially secure than the Mounts could be tempted.

'I think the club need to prepare you for that, and they don't,' he adds. 'You're watching a game and suddenly there's a guy talking to you and your wife. The next thing, he's putting his card in your hand and saying, "I represent this agency. I would love to meet with you and talk about us signing your son."'

To become an agent eligible to represent players within English football, the process is laughably simple with next to no barriers to entry. All one has to do is register with the FA as an intermediary, which requires the completion of a single form and the submission of a £500 registration fee, a basic criminal-record check and the upkeep of an annual renewal at the cost of £250 per year. Oh, and one must abide with the FA's 'Test of Good Character and Reputation', which amounts to little more than a commitment to comply with a set of loose conduct rules and a pinky-promise to not misbehave.

As of 5 January 2021, there were 2,439 names on the FA's list of registered intermediaries. The world of the football agent is one often painted as murky and deceitful, populated by exploitative ghouls out for a quick buck. This characterisation is unfair to the representatives who offer their clients proper care and advice, whether it be helping an international superstar negotiate a lucrative new sponsorship deal, or phoning round to find a club for a down-on-their-luck teenager released from an academy. But with such a large number of practising agents now within the game – most of whom hover around the bottom end of the intermediaries' hierarchy, with many hell-bent on becoming the next Jorge Mendes or Pini Zahavi – there are inevitably dozens of unscrupulous figures entering the world of youth football. They are competing like rival clubs to attach themselves to the coat-tails of the next big thing, to catch a quick, easy ride to the top.

FA rules outlaw agents from being able to sign players under the age of sixteen. But most parents of players within academies will have had several agents' cards pressed into their palms long before their son or daughter reaches that age. Between the ages of sixteen and eighteen, an agent can only sign a player with express parental consent. There are myriad stories within the game of agents attempting to woo the parents of standout academy prospects by any means necessary, dangling the offer of a mortgage pay-off or a new car.

'In reality, people that are driving round in cars and parents that have had their mortgages paid off, where has that money come from? It's come from their son,' Tony Mount says. 'It's payback. Some agents have got bad names. I know who they are, because you hear and parents talk. Some parents get in bed with them, and then within a year they've fallen out and want to get out of bed with them. It's a minefield. There is definitely room for [agents], but you've got to find the right one.'

'I think the biggest challenge is the parents,' Stephen Wright says of the sad reality he has witnessed in his time scouting for Liverpool. 'The one thing I do see is they're treating kids as meal tickets.'

***

'I knew I was shooting myself in the foot with the comments that I passed on to Ed Woodward, but I was at the point where I didn't care,' recalls Derek Langley of his final days as Manchester United's head of academy recruitment. A United supporter, Langley had been scouting young players for the club for sixteen years, having joined from Blackburn Rovers in 2000. He had risen to a role which saw him responsible for a worldwide network of around eighty scouts. His duties would take him far and wide – 'I was travelling all over the world, planes, boats, automobiles,' he says – identifying, tracking and, eventually, signing some of the world's best young players for the club. By the summer of 2016, though, he'd had enough. It wasn't that he no longer enjoyed the job, even if the travel was robbing him of quality time with his young daughter. It was that he had grown disheartened with how a once-slick operation had become hindered by red tape and the incompetence of those above him in the chain of command. He was sick of seeing other, quicker-acting clubs sign the players he was spotting. He increasingly felt undervalued by United's leadership, so he approached Woodward, the executive vice chairman, and delivered a few home truths. He was ready to fall on his sword.

'It had gotten to such a bad state, nothing was happening,' he says. 'You were banging your head against a brick wall. Every time I was putting players up for them, it was just a case of they were dragging their feet and putting so many processes in place. It was taking months and months and months to get any decisions off people. I'd been losing players left, right and centre. By that time, I just said, "It can't carry on."

'What made it worse was the fact that I was doing everything on my own. I had no assistance, no help. It got to the point where I thought, "Do you know what? I'm not even seeing my daughter grow up here. I'm missing all the quality time with her that I will never, ever get back." So I went in to see Woodward.

'He graciously gave all the members of staff fifteen minutes of his time, if you can believe it,' Langley says, sarcastically. 'I just told him that they'd got some very incompetent people working in the club, that were causing no end of problems. I said to him, "If you expect me to just come in here and say what you want to here, it ain't going to happen." Not many weeks later, I was relieved of my post.'

What Langley was essentially railing against was the further corporatisation of the club and the loss of expertise following the dual departures of long-time manager Sir Alex Ferguson and CEO David Gill in 2013. It used to be that Langley could approach Gill with sketched details of a target and, on the strength of the scout's recommendation, quickly get sign-off for an approach. And when attempting to convince a particularly sought-after youngster to choose United over any of the Premier League's or Europe's other elite clubs, he could knock on Ferguson's door and have one of football's most revered and successful figures sit the teen down and give a short history lesson. When Ferguson retired and Gill stepped down, the club's owners, the Glazer family, installed Woodward – a former investment banker who'd been pivotal in the billionaire Americans' acquisition of United in 2005 – as chief decision-maker and appointed David Moyes, who'd spent an impressive decade as Everton's boss, as manager. The old processes died.

'I'm not here to point fingers,' Langley says. 'With all the best will in the world, Ed Woodward is a fantastic guy, absolutely unbelievable when it comes to merchandising and financial implications – but clueless when it comes to football. You couldn't go to Ed Woodward and say, "I've got a player." He'd come back to you and say, "Right, go back to [head of operations] John Murtough; then go to the secretary; then go to [group managing director] Richard Arnold." By the time you'd finished, you'd have lost the player ten times over. This was the frustration of it all, because he was trying to delegate responsibility to all these people who themselves hadn't a clue on recruitment.

'Before EPPP came on board, we had a structure that was very sound, very solid. But we looked at it years before anybody else and had a think about the way that we needed to go for the future, by way of how we develop the kids, the coaching, accommodation, everything. And it was always hitting a brick wall. [Former chief scout] Les Kershaw had done a phenomenal job in identifying areas for new training complexes and development and everything, and none of them was interested. Sir Alex was – he was championing everything. But the minute Sir Alex left, all of this got swept under the carpet.

'We'd fought years and years for scouts' bonuses. The moment other personnel came in, they stopped all the retainers, they stopped some of the expenses. It just became a complete shambles. What they didn't realise is the core of the Manchester United staff were Manchester United people. They were stalwarts of the club. Now, you've got mercenaries in there. You can't even say they support the club. They like wearing the badge that says they work for Manchester United. If you ask them the DNA of a Manchester United player, they wouldn't have a clue.

'The very first meeting that David Moyes had was in the academy building, with every single member of staff of Manchester United there in attendance. That was all of them from Old Trafford, everybody from the academy, the Carrington training centre and everything – over 500 people. Richard Arnold put on a PowerPoint performance. It showed how many supporters we had worldwide, how big the club was, etc. etc. David Moyes then was asked to speak to everybody. The first words that came out of his mouth were, "I never realised how big a club this was." That was when everybody just looked at each other and thought, "This guy hasn't done his homework."'

The new regime, perhaps owing to Woodward and Co.'s background in the financial world, could still see the sense in recruiting continental talent early, though. The finalisation of the UK's exit from the European Union in January 2021 meant British clubs could no longer acquire players aged under eighteen from abroad. United made a concerted push to sign young players from EU countries following the Brexit vote in 2016 and before its eventual full implementation, maximising a potentially profitable market before the tap was turned off. A move to sign Dutch winger Tahith Chong from Feyenoord was wrapped up shortly before the referendum, but deals for Anthony Elanga, Arnau Puigmal, Matěj Kovář, Hannibal Mejbri, Dillon Hoogewerf and others followed. In the summer of 2020, the final pre-Brexit transfer window, United signed six teenage players – Willy Kambwala, Álvaro Fernández, Marc Jurado, Alejandro Garnacho, Isak Hansen-Aarøen and Radek Vitek – from EU countries. There is virtually zero chance of all these young recruits making a sustained impact at first-team level, but United know they can turn a profit on the players who don't make the grade, having recruited them relatively inexpensively.

The frequency with which United have been able to finalise moves for top European talent in the years leading up to Brexit's advent suggests the creaking internal mechanisms that so frustrated Langley have been greased and streamlined. But he found in his final months with the club that their push for the best continental teens could have been even more lucrative if these processes had been refined sooner. Langley cites former Ajax trio Matthijs De Ligt, Frenkie De Jong and Donny van de Beek as players he identified and proposed as targets long before their values soared following the Dutch club's Champions League semi-final run in 2019. His reports were never acted upon. De Ligt and De Jong joined Juventus and Barcelona, respectively, for a combined €150million; and United paid £40million to sign Van de Beek in 2020.

What most exacerbated Langley, though, was a deal United came much closer to completing. In 2016, they were deep in negotiations to sign Dayot Upamecano, a young French centre-back playing for Austrian second-tier side Liefering. Langley had studied the teenage defender for months, impressed by his speed, strength and comfort in possession. An agreement had been struck with Liefering for the boy's signature, and the player's family travelled to United's Carrington base for negotiations. After hours of talks, the terms of a contract were agreed. Everything was in place.

Or so Langley thought.

Instead of having the provisional agreement outlined on paper and committed to by all parties, Langley says the club secretary, John Alexander – the uncle of Liverpool full-back Trent Alexander-Arnold – made only a verbal, and therefore non-binding, agreement with the player's representative. Days later, the Upamecano family instructed new representation and returned asking for an improved offer. The deal fell apart and the player instead joined Red Bull Salzburg for €2.2million. Upamecano subsequently joined the energy-drinks manufacturer's Bundesliga outfit, RB Leipzig, before signing for Bayern Munich in a €42.5million deal in the summer of 2021.

'I'd spent eighteen months on that player,' Langley laments. 'I'd met his parents out in France. I'd been over there. I'd met the agent. I'd met the president of the club he was at. I'd done all the groundwork. Everything was done. And yet we could still cock the deal up after five hours of negotiations at Carrington. The secretary forgot to get anything signed, so it was all verbal. Two days later, the lawyer got sacked by the family, and a new lawyer was asked to renegotiate the deal. I asked the question of the lawyer. I said, "You weren't the lawyer who was here." He said, "No, they've employed me. The family want more payment." I said, "You can't do that, the deal has been agreed." He said, "Well, nothing has been signed." You can imagine my horror. I've gone back to the secretary and asked the questions. He said, "No, I didn't get anything signed." Two days later, he signed for Red Bull Salzburg. Now they're talking £50million for him. He was sixteen years old.

'That was why I left, because I just couldn't see a way forward. I was losing players, like the Ajax boys I've mentioned and quite a few others. This is the incompetence I was talking about.

'It was very much a frustrating time for me. After sixteen years, I just thought, "I've had enough now." They were killing me. When I finished, I would say a good eighty per cent of my scouts resigned. I used to be there at eight o'clock in the morning and I'd still be there at eight o'clock at night. But I'm out of it now. That's not my issue any more.'

Manchester United's scouts are, of course, not the only ones to have seen their pleas to sign star-shooting teens overlooked, ignored or fumbled by their club. Such is the industrial churn of young players these days, even the ones whose ability and potential are strikingly apparent occasionally go undetected. It is better to trawl the talent pool using a vast net with gaping holes, so the theory appears to run, than it is to cast a few reliable lines.

Martin Taylor was an academy scout for Chelsea for fourteen years, starting as a part-timer and rising to coordinate a fourteen-strong regional team, before spending four years in a similar role with Arsenal. He echoes many of Langley's frustrations over how future stars were missed through hierarchal lethargy. 'One thing that would disappoint me was when we'd have a triallist come in and we wouldn't even have him play a game,' he says. 'How can you see a player in a drill and not see him in a game? I think every player deserves that. If you get a trial at Arsenal or Spurs or wherever, you do deserve to have at least one or two games, just to see if you've got the ability to play that level. I was disappointed that sometimes Arsenal didn't do that.

'I saw Dele Alli when he was fourteen, playing for MK Dons. [Chelsea] said they had Ruben Loftus-Cheek at the time. They weren't interested. I highlighted him. If they'd have wanted him, they could have got him. The players Chelsea have had through the door but they've let go. They had Raheem Sterling at the club for a week. Chris Smalling they've had. [Sterling] came in for a week. He trained and trialled. The consensus was he was too small. He was at QPR at the time. They said he was too small. I didn't agree with that. Sometimes in the academy, the people making the decisions make the wrong decisions. They said Chris Smalling wasn't technical enough. I suppose you can say that in a way, but he ain't done bad, has he?

'I saw Jude Bellingham when he was twelve. You could see he was a player all the way along. I saw the boy Man United had, Angel Gomes, when he was twelve – I thought he was excellent. I highlighted all these players in my reports.'

The anguish Langley and Taylor express at seeing their recommendations ignored is rooted in how they feel football is evolving beyond their profession, pushing their expertise to the margins. The efficacy of their craft is built on trust, intuition and relationships. Their knack of identifying valuable traits within young footballers and predicting the future with as much certainty as fate allows has been honed over years of hard miles travelled, touchlines traversed. Now, thanks to data and video platforms such as WyScout and InStat, clubs rely increasingly on analyses conducted from afar. The old-school scout fights for relevance against laptop talent-spotters, who are often as young as the players they assess.

For the scouts already long in the game, adaptation is difficult. They barely recognise the new world they inhabit. They feel like master distillers who've been told their taste buds no longer know best; that the perfect whisky can be pinpointed by computer programme, ascertained by algorithm. Taylor maintains that there will always be a place for the eye test; that certain things on a football pitch can only be seen up close, in person.

'Scouting has changed,' he sighs. 'There's too much data. You see a player with your eyes. All the best computers in the world aren't better for spotting a player than your eyes.

'The first thing I look for is, can a boy handle the ball under pressure? If you can handle the ball under pressure, that means you've got a good intelligence of the game, because you might be surrounded by players, but if you watch good players – like Paul Scholes, Dennis Bergkamp – they receive the ball by letting it run across them. They don't actually touch the ball sometimes. It's just their spatial awareness. There's a saying I've heard: they smell the ball coming; they know the ball is coming, and they know what they're going to do with it before they've received it.

'Another thing I like in a player is a bit of character and desire. You see a lot of players that have got no intensity out of possession. I like to see players out of possession making runs, taking players away to create space. All those sorts of things. Too many players – even good players – are lazy off the ball; they'll only work on the ball. I think it's key that a player has some sort of intensity off the ball. Being two-footed really helps. Being technically clean is very important. And can you get around the pitch? Can you run? Can you move?

'I watched an Ajax session once. There was a guy putting on a session, and I asked him afterwards, "What is the Ajax way of playing football?" And he said, "TIPS. Technique, insight, personality and speed." That was their blueprint for a player. I've kept that in my mind a lot of the time when I'm watching a player.'

From the outside, scouting seems like the perfect job for a football lover. Scouts are paid to watch the game, travel the country and tick various stadiums and training grounds off their bucket lists. They are associated with professional clubs, claiming affinity with football's headline acts. But the reality is that a large majority of the hundreds of scouts working in the game do so only on a part-time basis, either paid a small retainer by their club or compensated based on the mileage travelled to each assignment. All eighty of the scouts who worked under Langley at United, for example, were part-time, and those Taylor oversaw at Chelsea held day jobs ranging from taxi driver to council worker to IT technician. The hours are unsociable, eating into weekends and evenings, and opportunities to climb the ladder are scant.

Scouts occupy arguably the most expendable position within the game. For most, they are bound so loosely to their clubs, through casual agreements or low-hour contracts, that they are readily and easily dispensed with when no longer of use. When Arsenal finished fifth at the end of the 2018-19 season, and as such missed out on a place in the Champions League for the third straight year, Taylor found himself out of a job.

'They said, because they didn't make Champions League, "We've got to make cuts to people's wages." They cut my wages in half,' he remembers. 'I'd put a really good team together. We brought in lots of players. Then the new regime came in. They brought this other guy in. They started redundancy proceedings. That was it. As cold and as callous as that.'

Within weeks of cutting loose Taylor and other staff, citing a need for belt-tightening, Arsenal agreed a club-record £72million deal with Lille for winger Nicolas Pépé.

'People think that scouting is quite a glamorous job, but clubs see scouts as ten a penny,' Taylor concludes. 'One goes out, another one comes in. That's how it is, how it's always been. I signed fourteen players for Arsenal in four and a half years, and they still made me redundant.

'Do the clubs really care? The answer is no.'

CHAPTER FIVE

RAISING A RASHFORD

'HOW CAN I help?' wrote Marcus Rashford when he first approached FareShare via email in February of 2020. The Manchester United forward had been inspired by the food-distribution charity's ActiveAte initiative the previous summer, which sought to supply food to vulnerable children during school holidays. He was concerned the looming pandemic would see yet more kids from low-income households go hungry in the months to follow.

'It's very rare to have an inbound offer, and an offer that says, "What do you need and how can I help?"' says Alyson Walsh, FareShare's commercial director.

By the end of June, Rashford had helped raise around £20million for FareShare, shattering his initial target of £100,000. He'd also lent his support to the Black Lives Matter campaign, spoken out against online bullying and successfully campaigned for the government to overturn its decision not to extend the free-school-meals scheme over the summer holidays and implement a £120million 'Covid Summer Food Fund' which reached 1.3million children.

Later in the year, Rashford conducted himself like an adult among squabbling children when Parliament, by a margin of 322 to 261, voted against a Labour Party motion to, as the footballer had implored, extend free school meals into October's half-term break and beyond. On several occasions, he appealed to MPs to put aside party politics and sniping for the greater good, aiming to smooth tensions more tribal even than those he overcame in earning the support of rival fans, players and clubs. He also took to social media to request that his followers refrain from directing abuse at these politicians, citing his own experience as a target for online bile as something no one should have to endure.

Inspired by Rashford's fight against child food poverty, and sharing his despair at the decision to curtail the scheme – which had provided meal vouchers worth £15 a week to children in low-income families outside of school term time – cafes, restaurants, pubs and even local councils around the country began to pledge to fill the gap. Rashford's Twitter timeline was alight in late October as he retweeted these organisations, notifying his followers of where the free food for the vulnerable could be found.

He was awarded an MBE in the Queen's birthday honours that month, to add to the PFA Merit Award and recognition from the Football Writers' Association, the City of Manchester and the Pride of Britain awards. Rather than allow these accolades to bookend a job well done, though, Rashford's admirable off-field work continued. In November, he forced yet another about-face from the government, with Prime Minister Boris Johnson personally calling the United forward to confirm a pledge of £170million to combat child food poverty through the winter and into the new year. This announcement came just days after Rashford teamed up with fashion brand Burberry to launch a series of initiatives to help disadvantaged people, including a

£25,000 grant to two youth clubs he attended as a boy and a donation to FareShare that would finance 200,000 meals.

In a letter to his ten-year-old self he penned for the campaign, Rashford wrote: 'For a young boy who says so little, one day you will have a voice that speaks for many.'

At the outset of the coronavirus pandemic, in April 2020, the UK's Health Secretary, Matt Hancock, took aim at Premier League footballers during a televised national briefing. Hancock suggested these high-paid sports stars ought to 'make a contribution, take a pay cut and play their part'. It was a craven attempt to deflect focus from the scrutiny the government's handling of the virus was beginning to draw, and to jab an accusing finger at a group often viewed by the wider populace as overpaid and underworked. Single-handedly, Rashford, through his social contribution and activism, made a mockery of the Health Secretary's swipe at footballers.

Rashford's efforts are informed by his own experiences. He spoke openly at the time about how important free school meals were to him as a child, and how hard his mother, Melanie, a single parent of five, had to work and budget to keep the family fed.

'It's definitely because he remembers his family, he remembers he was on school dinners and how difficult it was for his mum,' says Dave Horrocks, chairman of Fletcher Moss Rangers, Rashford's first grassroots club. And early signs of the conscientiousness and empathy that have marked out Rashford's activism can be found in his progression through United's academy. United make a concerted effort to instil such values in their youngsters – 'right is might', first coined by former director of youth football Jim Ryan, is an often-repeated mantra within the Carrington hallways. Politeness to all staff and visitors is demanded, and on tournament trips abroad, the boys take turns making speeches to thank their hosts, presenting pennants to opponents and gifts to hotel workers.

'Marcus would have had to do it a few times,' says Colin Little, the United under-18s coach. 'They all get a chance at it, to go and speak to the man in the canteen or go and give him a signed shirt. I'm sure other clubs are doing it, but when I got here, I'd never seen it before. You look at Marcus now, and you think, "Wow, what a good spokesman."'

But Tony Whelan, United's assistant academy director and one of the main drivers of the club's desire to develop empathetic individuals as well as top-class footballers, is quick to play down the academy's role in Rashford's inspirational off-field work. 'That comes from God, I think, a young man to do that,' he says. 'Obviously, he's had support and he's had role models – his parents, his mother in particular, and others. That comes from within, that comes from him. It's like your Mother Teresas of this world, your Dr Martin Luther Kings. People do some wonderful things, because somehow, within their being, God has given them that gift, and he has had that gift. So I don't think it's something that anybody else should take credit for in that sense.

'For us to see it with a young boy within our tenure at the club, those that have been around him and have had the privilege to work with him, it does give you a sense of pride. I wasn't expecting that when he was nine or ten coming into Man United's academy. We want him to go as far as he can, in terms of football and obviously be a really nice boy, and if he leaves us in the future, then he's going to go with a set of life skills that will help him on his way. We're not thinking he's going to be doing what he did, and being Dr Rashford at 22 [the University of Manchester awarded Rashford an honorary doctorate in July 2020] and doing just an amazing, amazing thing. It gives us a great sense of pride.'

Whelan is right to point out that Rashford's drive to effect real change on a national scale for those most in need goes far beyond anything United's academy coaches could expect their players to achieve outside of the game. But the club's 'right is might' philosophy provided a foundation upon which Rashford's charitable, empathetic and altruistic sides could flourish. While others might not go as far or do as much as Rashford, basic values of decency are taught and instilled in these young players as part of a holistic development package. 'Hopefully we created the kind of environment in which a young person could express himself in that way,' Whelan says. 'I think that's the thing. If we can set environments that say, "Look, nothing is impossible. You can achieve whatever it is you want to achieve in your life, whether it's through football or anything else."'

'Man United are, without doubt, the best at it,' Little adds. 'Tony Whelan and [academy player liaison officer] Dave Bushell are the fabric of the club. Paul [McGuinness, the former United youth coach] calls them guardians of the United spirit. If you've got a core of people pushing those values, you just keep drilling it home to them. It becomes the norm. Then Marcus takes on the mantle, and you see Axel Tuanzebe doing it. "Right is might" – it becomes who they are. They're so grounded, and it's because of the groundwork of Tony Whelan, Paul McGuinness in the past, and [academy manager] Nick Cox has carried on that work.

'It's not fake. It's real. It's not just faking it to show how good we are. And it's proof that Marcus has done what he's done now, caring about other people.'

Whelan, now in his late sixties, was a young player at United himself. He came through the club's youth system at a time when it was overseen by Jimmy Murphy, one of United's most revered and influential coaches, after whom their Young Player of the Year award is named. Although he never played a competitive first-team game, Whelan became only the second black player to represent United when he made his debut in a friendly in 1969. He later joined Manchester City and spent some time in American soccer. He retired from playing football in 1983, after suffering a broken leg while turning out semi-professionally for Witton Albion. From there, he made the curious career leap into social care, working with vulnerable children in Manchester. Whelan returned to United as a coach in 1990, and he has been a fixture of the club's youth set-up ever since. He has combined his coaching career with a thirst for learning, attaining an Open University degree in humanities and a master's in sociology from Manchester Metropolitan University. He then decided to pursue a doctorate as a means of professional development, an alternative, he saw it, to obtaining a UEFA Pro Licence coaching badge – 'That's for senior football,' he says. 'I work in youth football.' In 2015, he successfully completed his PhD, entitled *Pastoral Care of Premier League Academy Schoolboy Footballers*. Informed by his chosen topics of study and social-care background, no individual has had a greater influence over United's approach to rearing well-rounded youngsters within their academy.

'We've always believed that we had a responsibility to ensure that our young people grew not only as footballers but as human beings,' Whelan says, 'because at some point they are going to leave the club and, if they leave football, go into the wider world. So they need a set of skills – basic human skills that they need to survive and get on in the world. That was handed down to me from being at the club back in the day, from Sir Matt Busby, from Jimmy Murphy, from having to wear the club blazer, having to wear the tie, turning up properly, being respectful to people. I always remember going up to the laundry at Old Trafford when I was an apprentice, and the laundry ladies were like goddesses. You were told if you go and speak to the laundry ladies you had to be on your toes, you couldn't be disrespectful or not do what you were told.

'We were passing that on, making sure they follow in the footsteps. We made sure the young players, if they went on a trip, looked after the hotel, they knew how to look after their bedrooms. We used to tell them, "You're responsible for the rubbish in your room. When the cleaners come in, all they should have to do is change the bedding. That's it." And in and around the hotel, your pleases and your thank-yous, and training young people up to be able to give a speech to the head waiter in the restaurant at the end of a trip, to be able to present a pennant or a gift to the tournament organisers or the person that had been assigned to the team, making sure that they were being embraced and included as part of the family.

'We were always strong believers that it was important for them as young people to understand that being a footballer – particularly being a footballer at Manchester United and going on tour overseas with Manchester United – was a privilege and an honour and something that they should really treasure. And with privilege comes responsibility, the responsibility to do those things, because you're an ambassador for the club, you're an ambassador for football, and you're also an ambassador for your family. You want your parents to be proud of you. You want to be proud of yourself. And you want the staff at the football club to be proud of you because you've represented the football club in the right way. That's it, really. It's not rocket science. We've always tried to do that.'

The players lucky enough to maintain a place within a top-level academy, those who avoid being released long enough, have the opportunity to see the world. From as young as nine or ten years of age, children within United's academy will travel to continental Europe or even farther afield for tournaments. Whelan is keen to ensure that when the players visit far-flung locations, especially those rich in culture and history, they are able to remove the football blinkers, to see and absorb their surroundings.

'Whether it's a big city or a small village, there's somewhere that's the centre,' Whelan explains. 'We make a point of making sure we go there. I used to say in advance to our staff in the office, "What's the place? Where are we going?" We used to email ahead and say, "We'd like to go to such and such a place", to take the kids. You don't want them to go to a country just to play football. They've got to experience the country, eat the food, go and see the place. One of our junior coaches does a little booklet for the players, and in the booklet there will be little words and phrases and a little bit of history of the country, what's the food and how do you say "hello" and "goodbye", things like that. It's so educational.

'We went to Budapest with an age group. Ferenc Puskás, he was one of my heroes. I always remember thinking, "Budapest. Puskás. Wow." I remember saying to Claire in the office, "We're going to Budapest, can you ask if we can go and see Puskás's tomb?" We got a special pennant made that had his name on. We got there on the Friday, and the tournament was on the Saturday. In the morning, in the coaches' meeting, the guy said, "We've made an arrangement with Man United to go and see Puskás's tomb tomorrow morning if you'd like to join them." Everybody went. All the teams went. We go to his tomb. It's in the vault of this church. We lay our pennant. All the other clubs do the same. They made it a tradition. It was wonderful. To me, that's football. We had our photographs taken, and I treasure the memory, because that was educating a young person. You help to educate them about football then. You tell them about the England game in '53. You tell them this guy scored three goals. You tell them he scored three goals in a European Cup final, in the first half, and lost. You teach them not only about a great footballer, but about Hungarian culture. "This is where this guy was from. You've been to his grave. Where we're going to play, in this stadium, he played." You can't buy it, can you? And I'm in a privileged position to be able to do it. What a huge honour, and I'm always conscious of it.

'We tell our players all the time that you're following in the footsteps of these people. We have shirt presentations before tournaments, and we'll say, "Right, there's your shirt, you're following in the footsteps of Duncan Edwards, Bobby Charlton." We use it as an educational experience. It's an opportunity – don't waste it. Are we going to sit in a hotel room for four days and not teach them about football, not teach them about Man United, not teach them about culture – not only about the history of football and our football club but of the country they are in? To me, that's the absolute *raison d'être* of what we do. We wouldn't want to lose that.'

Whelan's commitment to providing an education for his players beyond the techniques and tactics of the game is born of the same protective instincts that saw him choose social care as a career after football, of his reverence for history and appreciation of the privilege of his position. But he also sees it as being indelibly connected to the primary concern of his role – to produce footballers for Manchester United, to raise more Rashfords.

'If you can improve them as a person, as a human being, you'll automatically improve them as a footballer,' he says. 'One of the problems we've got in our game is that we get it the other way around. I've always thought that if we sort the kid out first – the stuff that's off the pitch, get all that sorted out – the football is easy.'

***

'It was a relief,' says Greg Walters, describing his emotions upon learning that Aston Villa were not going to offer him a professional contract. A lifelong Villa fan, he was honoured and excited when he signed scholarship forms with the club as a sixteen-year-old. Walters's father had been friends with the late

Jim Paul, Villa's kit man of many years, and Paul would invite Walters to the club's Bodymoor Heath training ground to watch his heroes in action. He'd always dreamed of emulating those players, of adorning the claret and blue and feeling the Villa Park turf beneath his boots. In 1998, he was part of the first post-*Charter for Quality* intake of scholars – they were to be known as 'apprentices' no longer – and his ambitions at last felt tangible. Two years on, though, after constant verbal abuse and physical intimidation at the hands of the coaches who were supposed to nurture him, the news that the club he loved no longer wanted him was a sweet, welcome release.

In 2018, Villa launched an investigation into the conduct of long-time youth coach Kevin MacDonald after four former academy players alleged they'd suffered bullying and abuse at the hands of MacDonald and Tony McAndrew, another long-tenured youth coach who had left the club the previous year. Gareth Farrelly, one of the players to have raised a complaint, told *The Guardian* how there had been 'a culture of verbal and physical bullying', when he was a young player with the club in the 1990s, and that 'there were no checks and balances. [MacDonald] operated with impunity.' MacDonald was moved into a role which gave him no direct contact with players for the duration of the investigation, which was conducted by Jack Mitchell, an independent barrister. Villa declined to go public with the findings of the investigation, instead submitting Mitchell's report to the FA. The verdict on MacDonald's conduct was clear, though: he left the club 'with immediate effect' in August 2019.

'You didn't know what mood you were going to catch them in,' Walters says of McAndrew and MacDonald. 'You were scared of them.'

Walters struggled with injuries during his two years with Villa, and he remembers the two coaches being unsympathetic to his plight. In the training session after his first game for the club,

Walters felt a sharp pain in his shin. 'I think I need to go in,' he told McAndrew. 'Fuck off in, then,' came the coach's reply. Walters recalls being called a 'cunt' on a daily basis and how, whenever he joined in with training games, McAndrew would be a danger to the players he was charged with protecting.

'Tony McAndrew was only there in my second year. In my first year, it was Kevin MacDonald and [Gordon] "Sid" Cowans. Sid was fantastic. Sid would never call you a cunt. He was a proper footballer and he was a proper coach. He praised you when you did good things and he was on a level because he was a player.

'Tony McAndrew was a nightmare for us, and so was Kev. Kev was a little bit better. It was 1998, when money was starting to come into the game, and I think they were bitter.

'If you went into a fifty-fifty with Tony on the football pitch, he'd just smash you, and he did it on purpose. You dreaded going out to train. They were bullies.'

Defenders of McAndrew and MacDonald have pointed to the volume and quality of players to have graduated from Villa's youth ranks under their watch. The pair can claim a hand in the rise of England internationals Gareth Barry, Lee Hendrie, Darius Vassell, Gabriel Agbonlahor, Gary Cahill and, most recently, Jack Grealish. But Walters takes an opposite view. How many more stars could Villa have reared over the last thirty years had two of their most prominent youth coaches conducted themselves differently?

'You hear about players who practise, practise, practise, who stay out after training,' he says. 'I'd have loved to do that. We weren't allowed. If you'd have stayed out, Tony would have gone, "Who the fuck do you think you are? Get in, you cunt, and do your jobs." That's what it was like. If you tried to do something like that, they'd just belittle you.

'They were trying to make us into footballers, trying to coach us. They didn't need to break us. Why is this bloke, who's supposedly coaching me and trying to make me a better player, calling me a cunt and telling me I'm not good enough every day? They tried to break you, just because they could.'

Villa informed Walters that he would not be offered a professional contact three months before the end of the 1999-2000 season. Although he was keen to flee Bodymoor Heath by that stage, he still hoped for a future in football. He summoned the courage to approach his volatile coach in the training ground's gym and ask for help in landing a trial with Stoke City, where McAndrew had coached the previous year. McAndrew paused his workout, sat up from the chest-press machine, and laughed. 'It was like,' Walters says, 'he was taking the piss.'

In February 2006, almost four years after leaving Villa, Walters ran into McAndrew again. Jim Paul, the old, beloved kit man, had passed away, and Walters attended the funeral. At the wake, held in one of the bars at Villa Park, he saw McAndrew. Walters was instantly reminded of how small his old coach had once made him feel, of all the anguish he'd suffered. It crossed his mind to unleash on McAndrew, hold him to account for the bullying and intimidation. He weighed up the catharsis of a tirade against the embarrassment of breaking the peaceful remembrance of a departed family friend. Walters, by then, was already on a path to a successful career in financial services. Settling old scores, he felt, would serve no one. He opted for the moral high ground.

To his surprise, though, McAndrew approached him. 'I gave you a hard time,' the coach admitted. 'I was in a dark place myself.'

A step short of an apology, McAndrew's admission meant little. 'My time at the Villa wasn't good,' Walters reflects. 'It was a toxic environment.'

Greg Walters's experience at Villa is a world removed from the care, sensitivity and sense of duty with which Whelan describes his role at Manchester United. The kind of conduct McAndrew and MacDonald displayed is often excused as being 'tough love'. One former Villa player, regarded as a legend at the club, once countered Walters's recollections of the bullying he suffered by suggesting the coaches were merely trying to toughen the boys up. If they couldn't withstand such treatment on the training field, he reasoned, then they'd be ill-equipped to cope should they ever provoke the ire of a full stadium in the professional game.

Such attitudes, one hopes, are confined now to a bygone era. Sadly, though, what Walters and his team-mates experienced appears not to have been especially uncommon. Reports of similar behaviour – or even worse – have surfaced with time. In the early weeks of 2021, former Fulham academy player Max Noble spoke out about how he felt mistreated by his coaches in the mid-2000s. In an interview with the *i* newspaper, Noble alleged that he was the victim of verbal abuse and racism. 'We lost three or four games in a row and they said all of us had bad attitudes,' he said. 'The only ones that could train turned out to be the white guys. We had eight black boys in our team, the black boys in the afternoon would have to sit in the changing room while the three or four white guys would go out and train with the reserves.

'They wouldn't allow us to have lunch in the canteen, so made us sit in this dirty changing room after everyone had used it. There was mud everywhere and they would just put sandwiches on a tray on the floor for us to eat. That happened for two months.

'It's bullying – complete bullying. It's a horrible environment to be in where you're scared. I would tremble in the toilet.'

Noble also claimed to have been in contact with more than 150 former academy players who felt mistreated or abused within the system. Among them, he said, there have been multiple instances of suicide attempts, self-harm and depression.

There is also the sexual abuse scandal uncovered by journalist Daniel Taylor, now of The Athletic but reporting for *The Guardian* at the time, in 2016. Taylor's initial piece on the subject centred around an emotive and frank interview with Andy Woodward, in which the former Crewe Alexandra player waived his right to anonymity to speak out about the abuse he suffered while a young player at the club in the 1980s. Woodward's abuser, Barry Bennell, had been convicted of sexual offences against six boys and sentenced to nine years in prison in 1998.

In the days after the interview with Woodward was published, Taylor's phone was alight with more survivors coming forward. 'If I answered one call,' he says, 'I missed six others.' Over 100 more victims reported Bennell to the police for offences committed while he was employed by Crewe and Manchester City, leading to further charges and fresh imprisonment for the paedophile. Within six months, hundreds more victims felt emboldened to speak up, with allegations relating to coaches and scouts at over 300 clubs. Those included George Ormond, a former Newcastle United youth coach; former Chelsea scout Eddie Heath; and former Southampton and Peterborough coach Bob Higgins.

In 2018, the FA's independent inquiry found no evidence of an institutional cover-up within football. But at the time Taylor and one survivor of abuse at Crewe, Steve Walters, were interviewed for this book – more than four years on from the original flurry of allegations and charges – the FA still had not completed and made public the findings of the inquiry.

'It was disappointing,' Walters, a victim of Bennell's, says of the FA's response. 'I don't hold my breath, really, on the findings. My personal expectations are not high. A lot of the lads have already given up on it. If you set low expectations, you don't let yourself down. You gear yourself up for disappointment.'

Of the major clubs involved, Chelsea are the only one to have published a full, independent review into the allegations and how they were handled. Crewe initially committed to an independent review, but later shelved their investigations, claiming they did 'not intend to commission a further independent investigation to duplicate the thorough enquiries that have already been undertaken [by the police]'.

'As far as Crewe Alexandra are concerned, I've got no qualms about them any more,' Walters says. 'I'm prepared to move on. It would be nice to receive an apology or do something going forward with the club. The chairman still being at the club is still a bit of a kick in the teeth for the Crewe boys.'

'The reason they said they couldn't have an inquiry was because the police had already investigated and decided that there wouldn't be any more criminal charges,' Taylor adds, 'which was just bollocks. The idea of an inquiry is to find out how you can change things, for safeguarding. That isn't the police's job. The police's job is to look for criminality. I spoke to the police and they were privately furious about what Crewe had said.'

In the wake of football's historical sexual abuse cases being exposed, Steve Walters joined up with Woodward to found the Offside Trust. The organisation has the dual aim of eradicating sexual abuse within football and providing support for fellow victims.

'It was just a bolt out of the blue from Andy Woodward, the first survivor,' Walters recalls of how the idea for the Offside Trust was formulated. 'He approached me and asked me if I wanted to form some sort of group run by survivors for survivors of football abuse, and it all went from there, just trying to raise awareness.

'The ultimate goal is for what happened to us to never happen to any professional youngster again. Ideally, we'd like that to be any youngster at all, right down to grassroots level, but we soon realised that was going to be very difficult to do. It's the one topic no one wants to talk about in football. It's still a very difficult journey to go on, but it's one we're prepared to stick at.'

While the FA drag their feet in publishing the findings of

their investigation[1] into the sexual abuse scandal, there is at least now a recognition of past mistakes within youth football. More stringent safeguarding measures, mandated by the Elite Player Performance Plan, aim to ensure the game can no longer harbour predators. And there is a far greater appreciation of the responsibility each academy has to the wellbeing and development of the young people within the game. Too often in the past had the concept of 'tough love' veered from a necessary frankness into outright abuse and bullying.

'There is a greater level of mental health and wellbeing support for young people at football clubs than there is in any other sport, and I suspect most schools,' Nick Cox, Manchester United's academy manager, told Football365. 'Obviously, all this depends on what club you're at, and I acknowledge that at Manchester United we have more resources than most.' Cox was speaking during the coronavirus pandemic in 2020. In the midst of a national lockdown, United kept in regular contact with their academy players, checking up on how they were coping with the uncertainty and changing circumstances, sending gift packages and arranging for the kids to have video calls with first-team stars Jesse Lingard, Marcus Rashford and Scott McTominay.

It has gradually been recognised, also, that children who enter academies from eight years of age unwittingly sacrifice a chunk of their childhood toward the football dream. With such high dropout rates, there is a risk that, down the line, the many who don't graduate to a career in the game will feel they missed valuable developmental experiences for no reward. As such, many academies now are attempting to move away from a sense of early professionalism in the youngest age categories.

---

[1] The findings of the inquiry, led by Clive Sheldon QC, were released in March 2021, reporting "institutional failure" on behalf of the FA and condemning eight clubs for failing to react to reports and rumours of abuse within their organisations. A statement from the Offside Trust said of the report and its 13 recommendations: "The recommendations are ones which would have been blindingly obvious to anyone within a few weeks of the scandal breaking. The FA should have immediately made these most basic of changes around training, awareness, spot checks and transparency without waiting for a 700-page report."

'What we try and create here is to make sure that children are treated like children, not mini professionals,' explains Jon Pepper, Burnley's academy manager. 'Anything before twelve years old, it's fun, enjoyment, loving the game. We don't expect them to be drilled with lots of learning objectives and presentations, like our under-18s or -23s.

Burnley's young players aren't confined to hours upon hours of football practice when they turn up to the academy each week, either. Pepper has introduced a multi-sport programme which sees the kids try their hand at Thai boxing or tag rugby or gymnastics. In older age groups, as is increasingly common within other academies too, there are life-skills classes, teaching the players how to cook or manage their finances.

'If you're involved in an academy and you're coming here four, five times a week, you don't have the opportunity to do anything else,' Pepper says. 'You can't go and experience different sports. Kids don't play out on the street as much as they did back in the day. It's our responsibility to give them different experiences. Let them experience playing different sports.

'The younger ones, up to fourteen, follow the school year, so they have all the school holidays off, being kids, being with friends, going on holidays with their family. I don't want their childhood taken away because they've signed with an academy. I don't want unrealistic expectations on them. I want them to have a great time, because the stats say a lot of them will end up getting released. I want them to go, "I was at Burnley when I was a kid and it was fantastic." Academies get a lot of bad press. A lot of bad press. It's up to us. We hold the key to make sure they have good experiences, not all negative, because a lot of them were playing the game at a young age with their friends and then we drag them away to say, "Come and play for Burnley."'

When Pepper arrived at Burnley in 2016, he found the sessions being put on for the youngest age groups were intentionally trying to mimic what the under-18s and under-23s were doing. This, he felt, was no use. The majority of the players in the under-9s team are unlikely to make it all the way to the under-23s. And nearby super-clubs Manchester United, City and Liverpool are better equipped – in terms of player talent and staff experience – to offer hyper-technical training. Dialling back the intensity for the youngest players was part moral obligation, part competitive differentiation.

'We needed to be something different,' he says. 'We needed to create an environment where they come in and it actually feels different. Let's make the Foundation Phase the best grassroots club in the country, effectively, where it has that grassroots feel; family-oriented, loads of fun, big smiles on faces. When we get them into the building, no one really wants to leave, because they enjoy it.'

At Wolverhampton Wanderers, academy manager Scott Sellars espouses a concept he calls 'serious fun'. In nurturing a young player's enjoyment within the academy, he believes, you ring-fence their desire for the game and heighten their engagement.

'I want the kids when they're here to run through because they want to be here,' he says. 'Your first job as a coach is to engage with them and make it fun. In any education – because this is teaching, coaching is teaching – if you're not engaged or not having fun, or you don't feel that the teacher understands you, then I don't think you'll learn.

'When I was at school, we had an English teacher called Mr Chisnall. We used to walk in and he'd sit down, and he'd go, "Right, you've got five minutes, tell me a joke. Someone tell me a joke." So someone would tell a joke, then somebody else would tell a joke. Then he'd go, "Right, brilliant, really good. Now off we go to work." He had us like that, bang! Why? Because he engaged with us as people first, and then said, now we're educating. He made it about a relationship between people.

'What do they want? What do they need? That's your job as a coach. And that's what "serious fun" is about for me. Enjoyment. In that lesson, I learned, because I was engaged in that lesson by an English teacher, he engaged me as a teacher to [where I'd] say, "You get me, you understand me, and I'm going to do whatever I can, because you know that when I come in, you're going to let me have a bit of fun and we're all going to have a bit of a laugh, but I know when it's time to work." And hopefully they should know when it's really time to work now.'

Browbeating and bullying into obedience was once – and for too long – the coaching method *de rigueur* in youth football. There are other ways of raising young footballers, more respectful approaches that don't make collateral damage of the children eventually cast aside.

'Engage,' Sellars implores. 'Make it fun and let them learn.'

CHAPTER SIX

DEAR PARENT/GUARDIAN

1 OCTOBER 2020

[click or tap here to insert recipient's email address]

Dear parent/guardian

I'd like to thank you for your support during your son's attendance at our academy development centre programme. Having assessed your son during his time with us, we currently feel he is not ready to progress further within our academy development programme. Therefore, we are unable to offer further training at this present time.

Players develop and progress at different ages and your son has done extremely well to participate at the academy development centre. At such a young age, we do not offer individual feedback on the players. However, there are general areas of the game and techniques that all players can develop further, such as dribbling, passing, receiving, turning, one-v-one attacking and defending, first touch, weak foot, concentration etc.

We hope that your son enjoyed his time at the centre. We will continue to monitor his progress via our scouting network.

If there are any queries, please do not hesitate to contact us by email.

We would like to thank your son for attending our coaching sessions and we hope that everyone in your whole family's experiences were worthwhile.

Yours faithfully and kind regards

That, word for word, was the email sent by a Premier League club to the parents of seven-year-old Justin Broad. [At the family's request, the names of the player and his father have been changed here to protect the child's identity as he is still hopeful of progressing through the academy system. They have also asked that the clubs he played for are not named.]

Justin began dribbling a football when he was eighteen months old, says his dad, Simon. When he was three, he took part in a soccer camp while on a family holiday, and all the coaches remarked upon a preternatural talent. Simon loved football as a child, too, but his father never allowed him to pursue the game; academics were the sole permitted focus. When Simon's school asked if he could join their football team, his father's response was blunt: 'I send my son to school to learn, not to play football.' Simon resolved that if ever he had a child, he would throw his wholehearted support behind their passion, whatever it might be. So from the moment Justin showed an interest in football, Simon became, as his friends described him, a 'proper football dad'. A few weeks before Justin turned five, he was invited to attend a closed trial at the local development centre of one of London's biggest clubs. Simon wasn't going to hold his son back.

There were seventeen other infants at the trial. The coaches had the boys run through some ball-work exercises before competing against one another in one-v-one drills. Justin excelled. The coaches asked that he come back.

Justin supplemented his weekly training at the development centre by joining Lambeth Tigers, one of the top grassroots sides in London. Most of his team-mates at the Sunday-league club were on the books of professional teams, too. Within a year of his first sessions with the Premier League club, three more top-flight teams from around the capital showed interest in Justin. By the age of seven, he was training at four Category One academies or their closely affiliated satellite centres.

The boy's packed training schedule demanded a large chunk of his family's free time – travel to and from four pre-academy training sessions each week ate up most evenings, and that's before factoring in commitments with his grassroots club. But Justin was happy, and Simon had vowed not to hold him back.

In February 2020, during a training session with one of the London-based Premier League clubs, Justin battled for the ball with another seven-year-old. The pair lost their balance, entangled in a spirited tussle for possession. They fell to the ground. The other boy landed on Justin's leg, breaking Justin's tibia and fibula. He underwent surgery to realign the fractured bones the following day. Football had consumed his little life, but Justin would spend the next seven months recovering, unable to play.

Simon describes the support his son received from the club with whom Justin was training when he broke his leg as 'pretty shocking, in that it was none'.

'We have asked for an incident report, to understand what happened,' he says, 'and we still haven't got that.

'His first club, I was actually shocked by. Justin was still with them, but I was getting the impression he wasn't one of the most rated boys there, just because he wasn't getting opportunities to go to tournaments. He'd had some invites to go to their main academy site, but they had sent some boys up for six-week trials there, and he wasn't selected. When we contacted them [to tell them about Justin's injury], they were really apologetic, really sad for him. They said they would get in touch with their medical team to offer him some medical help and some physio once he was back on his feet. Then lockdown happened [during the coronavirus pandemic], and when I contacted them to get that support, it wasn't forthcoming.'

One of the other clubs with whom Justin had been attending regular sessions expressed sympathy upon hearing of his leg break, but their sympathy was followed by seven months of radio silence. Of the four professional clubs, only one kept in regular contact, even assuring Justin and his parents that the boy would be welcomed back after he'd recovered. They'd already seen enough, they said, to be convinced to offer Justin a place in their pre-academy side for the next season.

Justin returned to his first club, the one whose scouts had spotted him at four years old, the one with whom he'd committed at least one evening each week for almost half of his life. Three weeks after the boy had gone back to the development centre having made a full recovery, the club sent Justin's parents the email reproduced at the beginning of this chapter.

'The email wasn't personalised,' Simon rages. 'It was one of those that says, "insert email here", and they didn't even bother to do that. It wasn't addressed to us personally, so I guess it's some sort of generic email they send to everyone.

'This is part and parcel of the game. I know this is the harsh side of it. But what my missus was most upset about was, he has been with you since he was four years old, and he's now seven, going on eight. That's a big chunk of his life. We didn't even get a phone call or a personal message. We never had anyone to call us and say, "How has he been with his leg?" And not even a WhatsApp message or an email to say, "How has he taken the news?" or anything like that. He was totally discarded.

'After all that time, a boy that age would be disappointed. Especially as a lot of the boys you played with are in the same grassroots team as you. They talk about things they're doing at the club and where they are. It's going to be common knowledge you've been released. It's not something you can hide from. It is really competitive, the environment he's in. It's difficult.

'If you're not one of the elite boys, someone that they're banking on, then they just don't care, it seems.'

Simon broke the news to Justin gently, and the boy took it well. He understood that it was just the opinion of a couple of coaches that he wasn't good enough for their club, and that opinions can change. He has resolved to prove them wrong.

'We're trying to pick up the pieces and navigate through this whole thing,' Simon says. 'Still chasing the dream.'

***

The formalisation of the academy system, first through the *Charter for Quality* in the late 1990s and later refined further with the advent of the Elite Player Performance Plan, brought many necessary and welcome advancements in professionalism and player care. But it also industrialised youth development, drawing thousands of young people into a hyper-professionalised environment and injecting them with the notion that they are on a pathway to the Premier League. There are now around 12,000 players, from age eight to eighteen, contracted to the academies of English football's professional clubs. And that figure accounts only for those old enough to be formally signed. The very first pre-academy regulations were introduced ahead of the 2020-21 season, but there is still no minimum age at which professional clubs can invite children to train informally with them. The Premier League's development rules manual states clubs can have up to 250 players within their academy, but it does not stipulate how – or if at all – these players and their families should be prepared for the release that awaits the overwhelming majority of them.

Less than 0.5 per cent of under-9s within an academy will ever make even a single appearance for that club's first team. Between 500 and 600 boys are released by academies every year. More are sucked into the system in their place. The machine keeps churning.

Yet a scout from one of the four London-based Premier League clubs Justin represented felt it appropriate to gather the parents of a pre-academy side and make a wild assertion about the future their system all but guaranteed. 'We are considered elite,' the scout proclaimed. 'If you've been with us two years plus, the chances are you will be a professional footballer. It's a one-in-four chance you'll be selected by us. And if you're not, it's a one-in-two chance you'll be a professional footballer, because of the standards that we have.' It was a baseless, reckless statement. The aim was self-aggrandisement, but the true result was to instil false hope. It is worrying to consider how many more groups of impressionable young players and their often equally impressionable parents to whom this experienced and respected scout repeated their careless claim. It is irresponsible, in the full knowledge that release awaits the majority, and that most fall out of the game long before adulthood, to raise these children's hopes in such a way.

'There's no typical situation,' says David Wetherall, the former Leeds United and Bradford City centre-back who has served as the EFL's director of youth development since 2011. 'But, generally, in a lot of situations where the transition has been a bit of an issue is when it's come as a surprise to the player and to the family. We have systems in place for really regular feedback to the player and to the family, parent engagement. And hopefully that sort of mitigates that to some extent. The player and everybody around gets an indication that it's likely they're not going to be here next year, rather than everybody thinking they're doing really, really well and progressing fantastically well and it comes as a hammer blow and bolt out of the blue. It's important that we've got that feedback aspect so that everybody knows where everybody stands and things are not a surprise.'

There is, of course, no way of guarding against some degree of disappointment, and it's easy to imagine how proper feedback mechanisms and honest appraisals, as Wetherall outlined, would minimise the way in which release from an academy setting could feel like a callous, concussive blow for those discarded. But such measures don't appear to be as pervasive as one might hope and expect. That's certainly what Cheryl Thompson found to be the case when her son Marvin [again, the names have been changed at the family's request] was cut loose by Millwall.

Marvin was late to organised football by most children's standards, joining his first grassroots team aged twelve. He quickly displayed a natural talent for the game, though, and was signed by Millwall within a year. He spent eighteen months at the club's academy, making the forty-five-minute journey through traffic from his home in Dulwich, south London, to the training ground in Eltham for three sessions a week and a match every Sunday. Marvin's two sisters, fortunately, were understanding of his ambition and accepting of the amount of time it kept their mum occupied.

At the end of his first full season with Millwall, Marvin grew anxious when his team-mates had received emails informing them of whether they were to be released or retained. He hadn't yet gotten one. He badgered his mum to investigate, so Cheryl texted his coach. 'When he didn't reply,' she says, 'I knew that my son was getting released.'

The email came through the next day. Marvin was no longer wanted.

'I would have thought, with him being so young,' Cheryl suggests, 'that he would have been brought in, so that they could sit down and explain to him why he'd been let go, and whether there was anything he could improve. Marvin loves football. He eats, sleeps football. For him to be told he's not good enough, mentally he couldn't handle it.

'I just thought the club should have brought them in to let them down a little bit more gently. This was my son's first experience of being let go, being told, basically, you're not good enough. It hit him hard. It hit him really, really hard.'

Cheryl had been into the academy offices two or three months earlier for a feedback meeting. At no point, she says, did the coaches with whom she met indicate that Marvin was falling short of the required standards. 'The way they were talking to me, it was: he's cool, he's all good. For them to let him go, it did not correlate with what they were telling me two or three months ago. It was very impersonal.'

Having ignored her initial enquiry via text message, Marvin's coach called Cheryl after the release email was sent to offer some brief, broad-stroke feedback on which areas of the game her son needed to improve and why he was released. No one from the club followed up to check on the boy's wellbeing.

'When they were signing him, we were all in the office,' Cheryl says. 'Everyone was very excited, signing the papers. Then when they were letting him go, they did it by email. I didn't like that. I made the school aware of what had happened, because I knew it would change his mood in school. He would probably lash out if a teacher said something to him, properly lose it, when that was not what he was normally like. It was just because of how he was feeling.'

In the months after Millwall let him go, Marvin lost all interest in football. The sport he once loved carried too much associative hurt. Speaking shortly before Christmas of 2020, Cheryl advised that her son, now fourteen, had just started playing again with his grassroots team. He doesn't want to join another academy.

***

Membership of the Professional Footballers' Association is open only to players aged sixteen or over. Therefore, academy players are not able to become PFA members until they reach the scholarship level. The PFA does, however, operate an independent and confidential twenty-four-hour hotline, the Youth Advisory Service, for academy players and their parents. The service can offer advice and clarification on matters of protocol, contractual disputes or safeguarding issues – but the PFA can't act on a player's behalf to help resolve any issues. In the course of reporting for this book, a case was presented off the record of one parent who contacted the PFA's helpline with what was deemed a 'major issue', and they did not receive a response for seven days.

For the most part, then, players and parents are on their own when it comes to navigating the murky waters of elite youth football. That's why, in 2016, Pete Lowe founded Players Net.

'I felt that there was a place for this independent support service, so we created Players Net, and that's what that is,' Lowe explains.

Lowe spent thirteen years as Manchester City's head of education, and since leaving the game, he has sought to use his expertise and experience in high-end youth football to help those still in the system. Players Net, in its current incarnation, aims to provide a more bespoke, empathetic and responsive support service than anything else currently available to young players and their parents.

'In the time that I've left the game, I've started to get phone calls from parents and, every now and again, from staff who want to speak about confidential issues and didn't know how to deal with the issues inside of the club,' Lowe says. 'Parents would come with issues that were, without fail, complex. Complex in that their son was at a certain club and that they felt speaking out about what was happening with their son would create a fractious issue and would end up with their son being dismissed from the football club. So you can understand the parents' perspective.

'Sometimes they just want to ask for advice, but not to let the club know they've asked for advice. We've had many, many of those issues. The Premier League have set up what they call their Player Care Department. In a private meeting that took place, they said, "This will help." I said, "This will only help if the parents come and speak to you. And they won't speak to you."'

Lowe wants Players Net to grow, to be more proactive in the support they can offer and to be able to provide a wider-ranging service than his resources currently allow. But that will require input and acceptance from the game and its governing bodies. Despite his vast array of contacts in football and the weight of his experience, he has encountered nothing but closed doors. 'We've tried really hard for five years now to get funding from the game,' Lowe sighs, 'and we just can't manage it. We were asked by the Football Association to create a business plan, which is what we did. It was highly praised by the then-chief executive of the Football Association and one of his associates who joined the meeting. It included a whole set of figures for the running of its first year and into its second year, how the business would develop and what, exactly, the demarcation lines would be of that business.' Despite the positive feedback, the FA weren't interested.

'It can only better football if there is an independent set-up,' Lowe suggests. 'The Premier League and the FA will say, "We fund a very well-known player-union body [the PFA] who should be acting in this space." As two people from a major organisation told us, "We know they don't act in this space."'

'This is not a case of Players Net saying to the game, "You're not doing a good job." But you can't mark your own homework.'

Shanelle Edwards has had a similar experience in her efforts to generate support, momentum and funding from the game for her Extra Time initiative. Edwards's vision for Extra Time is that it becomes a two-tiered support system for players released by academies and their parents. It is inspired by what her son Dermaio went through when he was released by Liverpool in 2015 at age ten, and then again by Oldham two years later.

'He did take it really badly,' she says of Dermaio's Liverpool release. 'He didn't play football for five months. He did actually go back into another academy setting, which was Oldham. I was quite wary about him going back in, but he said, "Mum, I want to do it." About three or four months after he went to the Oldham academy, we had the parents' evening there, where he was told not to come back to training. It really, really knocked him.

'It was what he said that inspired me to take things further. It had been really out of the blue, him getting released. He came home and he ran in his room and shut his door. I could hear him crying. When I asked him what was wrong, he said his life was over. He was only twelve, and he was saying his life was over – for football? It quite angered and upset me. It made me think, "Imagine how many other children are out there who felt that way."

'The way that I saw it is that they still have a duty of care, these clubs. The way that they release these children – my experience with both these clubs was that it wasn't done in a way that we could mentally prepare as parents, never mind our child, for what was going to happen. There was a training session, the child has gone to training, and it has been said and done there. It is quite cut-throat.'

Liverpool had released Dermaio mid-season, in January. Surely, Edwards thought, as he had a contract until the end of the season, he was entitled to continue to attend sessions until then? She sought the PFA's advice and found that her son did have the right to go back, but Dermaio didn't want to return. All his team-mates knew he'd been let go. He couldn't face turning up for training knowing the club didn't want him and his friends knew he'd been dropped. But as far as Edwards saw it, for at least as long as Dermaio was under contract, the club owed her son something – if not football training, then some form of support.

'If a child is being dropped in January, it shouldn't be told to everybody else,' she says. 'They should be allowed to stay and do the full term of that contract. And if they're not, these things should be implemented to try and motivate their mind during that transition period, because I feel like, for the child, it can feel like a bereavement. They've lost something. They've lost that identity. They've lost their group of friends and the training.'

Edwards formulated her idea for Extra Time in an effort to fill the gaps in the aftercare Dermaio had – or, more accurately, hadn't – received from his clubs.

'I started thinking about how there needed to be a service for when they let go of them,' she says, 'whereby we could support their health and mental wellbeing, with counselling if it was needed, and ways to develop resilience and strategies of coping with the negatives.'

After his release by Oldham, Dermaio was invited back to his old grassroots club, Fletcher Moss Rangers – who count Marcus Rashford and several former Manchester United players among their illustrious alumni – to coach the six-year-olds of their Saturday Soccer School. Edwards found this to be restorative to Dermaio's confidence and so decided to incorporate a link-up with affiliated grassroots teams into the service she would like Extra Time to provide.

'My plan was to try and work with the lower leagues and the grassroots teams to develop a package that could be added into the [academy] contract where parents and children could access the service,' she says. 'There's two tiers. The one tier where there's a support figure who's been through the process, where you do almost like a one-to-one, an action plan, where after a chat with the mentor they can signpost them on to what other support [they might need]. And having somebody to act as an advocate for the parents and the player, helping them get back into football or whether they want to try something else.

'The second tier would be looking at training and development and their emotional health. It all depends what age they are when these things are happening to them. The social aspect, to me, is a big thing, meeting people again and trying not to be isolated. Once they've come out of that academy, they're unlikely to still be communicating with the football friends they made while they were there. It's about trying to create a pathway. If we add in Extra Time when they've been released, it also helps build the club's reputation. They can say that they've put somebody on to a mutual, separate service. It maintains the club's reputation. It helps maintain the relationship.'

Edwards is still working towards setting up the service she envisages. She initially approached the Prince's Trust – a UK charity aimed at helping eleven- to thirty-year-olds with, among other things, financial support for starting businesses – but was unable to get funding because, she says, she was almost thirty and her idea was for a service rather than a product. And, like Lowe and Players Net, every effort she has made thus far to generate support for her initiative from within the game has been stonewalled.

Journalist David Conn has reported extensively on youth football and its duty-of-care shortcomings in his work for *The Guardian*. He is of the belief that, if they are not prepared to embrace and fund outside help such as that offered by Players Net and Extra Time, football clubs must do a better job of preparing young players for the likelihood of release, and let them down more gently when the time comes.

'People sometimes say it's the same in all elite sports, and other elite activities for young people, such as dancing and music,' Conn says. 'Young people can be selected very young, and all these activities have a high dropout rate, so I do understand that point: there is disappointment built into many activities for people who set their sights on turning professional. But in football, there is a very uneasy sense of youth development having been industrialised. We accept that clubs are much more sophisticated than they used to be, that there are good people working in academies and some good processes, but the worry is that it's a crushing-of-dreams factory. The vast majority devote their youth to it but not make it as professionals, so how much are they prepared for it? Given the resources in football now, many people feel that surely they can have more in place for the overwhelming majority of young boys whom they're going to release.

'I think you have to look at this from the perspective of the majority: this is a system that takes in hundreds and hundreds of boys at a very young age and then releases them. That is the system. If it's ninety-plus per cent, then surely that's the way to look at the system; not to say that the very few who do become elite professionals, Mason Mount, Tammy Abraham, validates it all. It must be recognised that this is a system that takes in so many boys, who mostly do receive high-quality football training but who also make very extensive sacrifices, then it doesn't lead them to a professional football career and delivers a very powerful rejection at a vulnerable age. The system is taking them all in and releasing them, so it should be judged for the outcomes and care it provides for those young people.'

With such high dropout rates, the stark reality is that football academies are dream factories only to the fortunate few who make it through. For most, they manufacture heartbreak. How that heartbreak is delivered and whether or not those let go are properly cared for, still, in spite of all the protocols and processes, is too often an afterthought.

CHAPTER SEVEN

HOW MANY TIMES CAN YOU FACE REJECTION?

DOWN THE STEPS of the pavilion, the central hub of Crystal Palace's academy site, turning right past where the under-23s had zipped through an intense morning session, and over to one of the outer pitches on which a dome-covered artificial surface will soon be constructed as part of a Category One upgrade, Paddy McCarthy is observing his under-18s. A member of the grounds staff ambles past on a ride-on lawnmower while former Portsmouth striker Svetoslav Todorov is leading the players through a small-sided, *rondo*-style possession drill. The aim is for the five players on the outside of the square and their one man in the middle to complete as many passes as possible. Five defenders buzz around, hustling to intercept, deflect and pressurise; misplace a pass, and you swap roles with one of the defending players. McCarthy stands on the edge, feeding balls in immediately after every out-of-bounds pass, keeping the intensity high. Todorov shouts the count: 'One! Two! Three! . . . Twenty-two! Twenty-three! . . . New ball!' An errant no-look pass lands one over-confident youngster into the middle;

"Argh, fuck!" shouts another as his lofted pass is too high, too long and too cute.

McCarthy is in his third season as Palace's under-18s manager. The former Palace defender and Republic of Ireland international counts Pep Guardiola as a major coaching influence, hailing the Manchester City boss as possibly the greatest football manager the game has seen. But he is careful not to try and emulate the Catalan. 'If I try to be Guardiola, it won't work and these players will see through it,' he explains. 'You have to be yourself. I try to learn from every coach – the good and the bad; learn what works and what doesn't.'

The squad for today's session is depleted of some of its more gifted players, owing to those who were drafted into the under-23s for a game the previous evening having been allowed a day's rest. Even so, McCarthy is less confident in his current crop than he was in his league winners of the season before. 'We had leaders,' he says of last year's team, the best of whom are now with the under-23s. 'Lads who would call each other out. You need that, because when they go up to the under-23s, it's quicker. They'll get told if they're not up to standard. They might fail at first but they'll learn from it. These players have so many different voices these days – family, agents, the media, social media. They have to understand who they need to be listening to: the coaches.'

Once Todorov's fast-paced ten-minute drill is over, McCarthy takes the lead. There is another short, intense drill. Miniature goals are placed at each corner of a twenty-metre-by-twenty-metre square and the lowest-scoring team is punished with press-ups. The session will then conclude with a six-a-side match on a shortened, thirty-yard pitch with full-size goals. The boys are competitive, prepared to reprimand one another when mistakes are made, and desperate to win. McCarthy regularly halts play to impart wisdom. 'In little games like this, good and bad habits are developed,' he tells his players. 'You're not going to defend like that in the eighteen-yard box in a game if you don't do it here.'

Andy Hinks, the club's lead academy sports scientist, stands at the side of the pitch. He is monitoring a tracking device into which information is fed from the GPS vests worn by the players. Hinks joined Palace in 2011, initially as an intern, and has seen the leaping advances in sports science first-hand. When he started, heart-rate monitors were the height of sophistication. Now, the players' vests relay detailed information about intensity and workload, using leased equipment from market leaders StatsSport. Palace have had GPS tracking since the 2013-14 season, he says, and the use of such technology at under-16s and under-18s level is a prerequisite of EPPP Category One status. Data on each player is pulled through in real time, with detailed 'loading' reports provided to coaches. They will then adjust each individual's programme for the coming week, depending on how much and how hard the data says the player needs to work – some might need to be pushed; others might need to dial it back. The players are sent a simplified version of the reports to their personal tablets, too. Anyone not pulling their weight has no escape and no excuse.

'Some managers are more receptive than others,' Hinks says of the technology. 'Sometimes it can be used as an excuse,' he suggests, implying the data can be appropriated by unscrupulous coaches to explain away failures on the pitch. 'Work with the ball,' Hinks insists, 'always takes priority.'

Between the pitch where McCarthy's session is taking place and the pavilion reside two small temporary buildings. The first one serves as an office for academy staff and the second as a classroom. It is compulsory under EPPP that academies offer higher-education studies, be that on site or within affiliated schools and colleges, to players aged sixteen to nineteen on scholarship contracts. Predominantly, the boys are enrolled on

A seventeen-year-old Tony Whelan (third row, far right) lines up alongside such Manchester United legends as George Best (second row, second from left), Denis Law (front row, third from left), Bobby Charlton (front row, fifth from left) and Sir Matt Busby (front row, far right) in August 1970. *Alamy*

An aerial view of Manchester City's purpose-built Academy Stadium and the bridge connecting the academy facilities to the Etihad Stadium. *Alamy*

Bury's decaying training ground in the months before the club's collapse.
A silhouette of the club crest of Manchester City, the previous residents, is still visible.

Nabil Touaizi celebrates putting Manchester City 1-0 up against Liverpool in the 2019 FA Youth Cup final. *Getty Images*

Academy Director Alex Inglethorpe addresses Liverpool's players after their penalty shootout win over Manchester City in the 2019 FA Youth Cup final. *Getty Images*

Phil Foden's first-team breakthrough gives hope to Manchester City's academy stars. *Getty Images*

For fifteen years, the grand manor house at Lilleshall, Shropshire, played host to a yearly intake of talented boys as part of the FA's National School programme. *Alamy*

Future England internationals Michael Owen (front row, far left) and Wes Brown (back row, sixth from left) were among the graduating class of 1996 at the Lilleshall National School. *Alamy*

The hoarding lining Crystal Palace's academy pitches makes clear their local pride.

Crystal Palace considered releasing Aaron Wan-Bissaka at fourteen.
By twenty-one he was their first-team Player of the Year. *Getty Images*

Mason Mount's parents were once offered £200,000 by an agent for the right to represent their son. The offer was firmly rejected. *Getty Images*

Rhian Brewster left Chelsea for Liverpool at fourteen. Other clubs tried to sway the player's father with a glimpse into an opulent lifestyle. *Getty Images*

Bayern Munich have chosen to no longer recruit in the youngest age levels. *Alamy*

Manchester United agreed to sign gifted French defender Dayot Upamecano as a teenager. The deal fell through due to internal incompetence. Having since joined Bayern Munich, Upamecano is one of Europe's best young centre-backs. *Getty Images*

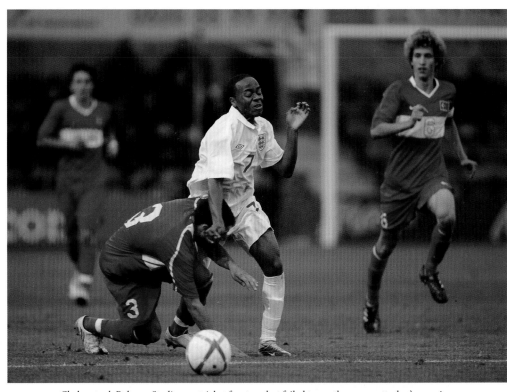

Chelsea took Raheem Sterling on trial at fourteen but failed to see the young attacker's promise. They ignored a recommendation to sign Dele Alli at the same age, too. *Getty Images*

Marcus Rashford's social conscience was allowed to flourish within Manchester United's academy. *Alamy*

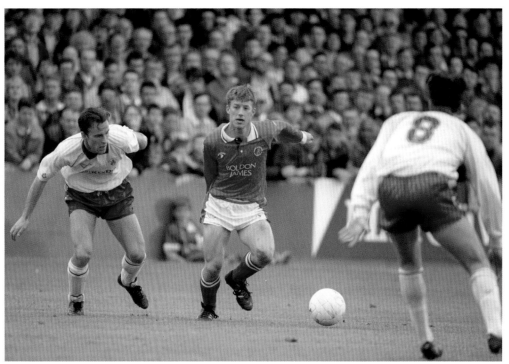

Steve Walters (centre) was a victim of sexual abuse while a young player at Crewe Alexandra. He has since founded the Offside Trust to ensure better protections are put in place for today's academy players. *Alamy*

Scott Sellars introduced his concept of 'serious fun' to the Wolves academy. 'Make it fun and let them learn,' he implores. *Getty Images*

The parent of one Chelsea youngster explained how his seven-year-old son was released via an impersonal email after suffering a broken leg. 'If you're not one of the elite boys,' the player's father says, 'then they just don't care.' *Getty Images*

Scott Armsworth (pictured tackling Arsenal's Matt Smith) felt the support he received after being released by Fulham was inadequate. 'How many times can you face rejection?' he ponders. *Getty Images*

'Exit trials' offer released players a chance to find a new club, but these mass auditions have been likened to a cattle market for young footballers.

Trent Alexander-Arnold's conversion from midfielder to right-back was carefully designed by Liverpool's youth coaches. *Getty Images*

Liverpool's sprawling Category One academy is adjacent to the club's new first-team training ground. *Alamy*

Marcus Rashford takes on Leicester City's youngsters as an undersized under-18s player. *Getty Images*

Rashford's dream first-team debut saw him score twice against
FC Midtjylland in the Europa League in February 2016. *Alamy*

Liverpool Women's academy manager Julie Grundy provides a
history lesson on female football's pioneers at a local primary school.

QPR coach Manisha Tailor was awarded an MBE in 2017. *Alamy*

Modern facilities blend with an old-fashioned ethos at Burnley's training ground and academy.

Losing Ian Carlo Poveda (above) to Manchester City, along with Joshua Bohui's departure for Manchester United, convinced Brentford to shut down their academy programme. *Getty Images*

Colin Gordon (left) wanted Kidderminster Harriers to become a hub of opportunity for young people, with grand plans for the club's academy and a university programme. *Getty Images*

David Longwell implemented lessons learned from La Masia at Shrewsbury Town's academy. *Getty Images*

Marcus Rashford's first-team breakthrough at Manchester United was the result of hard work, sacrifice, careful planning . . . and an all-important dose of luck. *Getty Images*

BTEC Sports Diploma programmes, with the qualification deemed a fall-back option for those who don't ultimately achieve a career in the game. The necessity for a viable plan B is laid bare by research conducted by the PFA which found that five out of six players offered scholarship deals are no longer playing professional football by age twenty-one.

Palace's planned academy redevelopment will include the instillation of purpose-built classrooms. For now, though, this hollow, echoing annex, kitted out with sixteen top-of-the-range Macs, is where Martin Prickett, the club's head of education, is attempting to teach a lesson on the muscular system, encouraging seven distracted boys to put together a Power Point presentation. 'Come in,' he instructs the teenagers, who each shake his hand on their way. 'Put your phones down.' The boys don't misbehave, *per se*, during the class, but their attention for non-football matters is limited. Prickett, who used to work in a similar role for Watford, describes the crux of his duty, to engage these young athletes, as 'nigh on impossible'. Education is provided. Inspiration to fully absorb it, to consider the likely need for future planning that doesn't culminate in a professional football career, is another matter.

During McCarthy's session, one player stands out above his peers. Tall and sinuous, his physique and easy leadership is reminiscent of former Arsenal captain Patrick Vieira. He pops passes between gaps in the defensive unit, and when hunting the ball he is focused, determined, instructing others where to go. He cajoles those around him and is visibly frustrated if his touch is less than perfect or one of his passes misses its mark. His name is Martin Onoabhagbe. He is the captain of Palace's under-18s and appears frequently for their under-23s. A relative latecomer, he was plucked from local grassroots football and drafted into the academy at under-16s level, raw but with evident potential. He had worked hard and developed well over the past two years, confident enough of his belonging at the level that leading this small group of eighteen-year-olds comes naturally.

Less than a month later, Palace released Onoabhagbe.

'To be honest with you, I had a sneaky feeling that they might let me go,' he reflects. 'In my second year as a scholar, the beginning was really great. I was captain. We were winning games. I was getting regular minutes with the under-23s. Then, towards Christmas, I started to see a change. I wasn't with the under-23s as much and, even though I was playing with the under-18s, I got the feeling that maybe I wasn't being looked at as much.

'Another thing that sparked my mind was my agent had a talk with Paddy [McCarthy] about how it was going with the pro contract. I remember him telling me what Paddy said was: right now, they're not too sure; it's fifty-fifty and they were OK with me looking elsewhere. That alone gave me some sort of indication that maybe they didn't want me.'

Onoabhagbe took both his parents with him into his appraisal meeting with McCarthy and academy manager Gary Issott. The coaches told him that, technically, he was still a little too raw, and that there were players in his position in the age groups above and below him whom they considered better prospects. He was welcome to continue to train with Palace until the end of the season, they said, but he wouldn't be coming back beyond that. There would be no professional contract.

'At the end of the day, it's still never nice to hear,' Onoabhagbe says of the let-down meeting. 'You feel like you're unwanted. At the time, I remember myself being very distraught, upset for a couple of days. But I knew I had to push on. Obviously, Palace didn't want to give me a contract, but I thought maybe I could get a contract somewhere else. I had to do something.'

Some of Onoabhagbe's team-mates who'd suffered a similar fate fell away, electing not to return to the scene of their heartbreak to continue training at the academy. Onoabhagbe saw out the season, though, training several times a week, mining McCarthy for any final nuggets of insight that could aid his chances elsewhere. He'd run and lift weights when he got home, too, in a desperate effort to be ready for whatever opportunities lay ahead.

'I believe we were told in March,' he says. 'We had a couple of months to figure things out. It would have been better to hear a little bit sooner because a lot of clubs were looking at giving [professional contracts for the next season] already and making their decisions. As players, it probably would be better if we were told even one more month in advance, so we can start preparing ourselves for whatever is going to be next.'

Injury curtailed a trial with Colchester before the season's end, and Onoabhagbe went into the summer of 2019 unsure of what was next for him. No contract. No club. Few prospects.

He accepted an invite to attend the Premier League Pre-Season Camp, a week-long training programme for twenty recently released players. There were sessions run by top-level guest coaches, fitness and conditioning work and several seminars aimed at broadening the teenagers' horizons within and beyond the game. It was explained to the boys how they could look to rebuild their careers in non-league football, or even apply for a scholarship to attend an American university.

'It was basically a camp to tell us that there were still options there and to not be helpless,' Onoabhagbe says. 'I thought it was a good idea. I actually got back in touch with the Premier League and asked them if they could possibly help me apply to go to America on a scholarship. I ended up taking my SATs. I did OK in that, but, in the end, I decided to not go, reason being I was looking over the information about players who actually make it over there in MLS, and it seemed there was a slimmer chance of making it over there than I would have over here. The best chance for me would be to go into non-league, gain some experience in men's football and work my way back up the ladder.'

The Covid-19 pandemic cut short promising spells with Cray United and East Thurrock in the seventh tier. The season was abandoned and Onoabhagbe was left wondering when he'd next be able to play, and whether his new club would even survive the financial hit caused by the coronavirus shutdown. Rather than linger in limbo, Onoabhagbe called time on his football ambitions. He enrolled at St Mary's University, Twickenham, to study sports psychology.

While the Professional Footballers' Association can offer little help to most academy players, as members must be at least sixteen years old, any player to complete a scholarship at a professional club is entitled to lifetime eligibility for grants to help fund further education, irrespective of whether or not they've ever played even a minute of senior football. The PFA currently provide financial aid for academic and vocational qualifications to 1,500 players – all of whom pass, assures PFA director of education Pat Lally, as the grant money is only released once the player has completed their chosen course. The organisation commits a yearly budget of £2million to educational grants and runs a 'transition programme' throughout the year, visiting clubs to talk to under-23 players about their next steps outside the game and to make them aware of the help on offer. Upon deciding to pursue a degree rather than a career in the lower leagues, Onoabhagbe was put in touch with the PFA and informed he could tap into a bursary.

'We had one young man who left the programme and went on to a scholarship in America; he went to Harvard University, ostensibly to continue his education but the university wanted him to play for them as well,' Lally, a former professional player with Millwall, York City and Swansea, boasts of his organisation's post-football success stories. 'At the end of his four-year degree programme with Harvard, he came back to England and went to Oxford for a year, to do a master's. Then Harvard invited him back to do a PhD. He qualified last summer as an orthopaedic surgeon.

'We've also got another young man who we provided funding for who is now a first officer for EasyJet. He qualified as a pilot. We currently run a number of discreet programmes ourselves in physiotherapy and sports journalism. We virtually fully fund those programmes – of the £9,000 that it costs, the PFA provides £7,000 per individual to fund those courses. The results that we've had from those courses have been phenomenal over the years.

'We've got lads that have qualified as physiotherapists, journalists – [Sky Sports presenter] Scott Minto was probably one of the more high-profile lads who came through our journalism course; [former West Brom, Leeds and Derby striker] Rob Hulse is probably one of the more high-profile players who came out of our physiotherapy degree, and is now working out of a hospital in Birmingham. We've got lads that are forensic scientists, podiatrists, lawyers. We've also got lads that have taken less high-profile qualifications, such as a lad in Bournemouth a couple of years ago who saw a niche in the advent of so many people buying wood burners; he trained to become a chimney sweep.

'If you name an industry out there, there's probably a player in that industry, and they will have received funding from the PFA in one way or another.'

Lally also lists dog groomers, wine merchants and clergymen among the game's alumni the PFA have aided in finding new careers post-football. But the PFA's outreach efforts don't reach everybody who needs them, it seems; at least not in as meaningful a way as is often required. Scott Armsworth still receives impersonal emails from the PFA, but never a phone call or any face-to-face interaction with one of the association's representatives. He was given no counselling on his transition, before or after he was released by Fulham in 2019.

Armsworth hails from a military background. With his dad in the army, he moved around a lot as a kid, never in one place long enough to lay deep roots. So when, at age fifteen, he was scouted playing locally in Aldershot and offered the chance to join Fulham's academy, leaving his life behind to chase a dream he'd begun to believe was beyond his reach didn't require a second's thought. 'It was a dream come true, going into that environment,' he says. 'I always knew going into the system would be hard for me. I was an underdog. I was never going to be technically as gifted as some of the other lads who had been in the system a lot longer than I had or were just naturally really gifted. I knew it was going to be hard work, but it was one of those opportunities you could never turn down. It was an opportunity I was willing to give my all at.

'I was over the moon. It was a stepping stone for my career in the game, which was great. A big thing for a lot of the lads is that it's your first time moving away from home. You're stepping out of your comfort zone. It's a big jump in terms of independence and looking after yourself, and maybe not speaking to your family as much or seeing your friends outside of football. You're pretty much twenty-four-seven in the zone of football. But it was my dream, I was buzzing.'

Armsworth played only sparingly for Fulham's under-18s during the first year of his scholarship. The majority of his team-mates had been in an academy environment most of their lives by that point. He was a willing, dogged, committed centre-half, but unrefined compared to his peers, locked in a constant game of catch-up. In his second season, he found his groove. He began to play regularly for the under-18s, a commanding presence having found his voice and a confident contributor in training and matches. Still, as the decision over whether or not he'd be offered a professional contract loomed, he grew apprehensive.

'That was a really difficult period, the two-year scholarship,' Armsworth remembers. 'I was always chasing what was in front of me, going into training knowing I was always going to have to apply myself 100 per cent, when others might have been taking it easy or having a laugh. I had to make sure I was doing everything that I could to develop.

'At the end of the scholarship, it was a difficult one, because I didn't know what to expect. All in all, I'd had a fairly good second season, so I didn't know what to expect in terms of whether I'd be offered a third-year scholarship or a professional contract. Unfortunately, it didn't go my way.'

When Decision Day came, in late March, the second-year scholars were all in the gym at Fulham's academy facility. One by one, they were called into the office within the adjacent pavilion building. They were met by academy manager Huw Jennings and the two under-18s coaches, Colin Omogbehin and Steve Wigley. After each player was given the news of whether they'd be returning after the summer, professional deal secured, or released at the end of the season, they would walk back across to the gym, either elated or crestfallen.

Armsworth quickly got a sense of the bad news awaiting him. The tenor of his conversation with the coaches was more *So what's next for you?* as opposed to anything that suggested his future remained in south-west London.

'It's a huge blow, being told you're not good enough,' he says. 'You have to get your head around the initial negative thoughts – "Why am I not good enough? What more could I have done? Why don't they want me here?"'

The coaches made a point of stressing how well Armsworth had done to come as far as he had, acquitting himself well among players who'd been in the system much longer. They told him what an asset he'd be to other clubs. It was little consolation. Armsworth was crushed. And confused.

'The football industry is very cut-throat,' he says. 'It is a very lonely period. You're not certain what's going to happen next, and that's the scariest thing – where will I be next season? Am I going to fall out of football? What am I going to do for work? After that period of rejection and negativity, it can be heart-breaking.'

Armsworth hadn't previously bothered with agents; he hadn't wanted one, and they hadn't shown much interest in him. When his name appeared on Fulham's list of released players, though, the agents soon came calling. He instead leaned on Jennings's support. The academy manager kept in touch and helped arrange trials at other clubs, but Armsworth, still reeling from the news his prospects with Fulham had ended, found it difficult to perform. The first trial set up for him was with Colchester, a week-long try-out. Anxiety began to take grip. He'd worry not only about how he'd perform in the sessions but also over whether he might get caught in traffic and arrive late. 'You're completely out of your comfort zone when you go on a trial,' he says. 'Everything is just running round in your head and it's all negative. You don't know what to think. You had to just focus on playing football and ignore everything around you, all the negative thoughts.'

Still, he managed to stave off the dark thoughts and enjoy his week with Colchester. After a brief, unsuccessful trial with Crystal Palace, Armsworth was invited back by Colchester for another week's try-out. He took heart from the fact the Essex club wanted a second look at him and felt cautiously confident he'd found a new home. But the week ended in another knockback. 'I've gone from Fulham to Colchester, and I still can't get a professional contract – that sort of thought was circling around in my head,' he says.

An intense training period with Brentford's B team was next. Another rejection. Then Watford. Another rejection, this time the bluntest of all – 'Watford, to me, felt like a waste of time. It felt like they didn't want me there. It felt like they were just doing a favour almost. I turned up and there were five other centre-halves there.'

Including Fulham, five teams had told Armsworth he wasn't good enough for them in the space of just a few weeks. The anxiety of having to impress would build with each trial, and crushing disappointment had now come to feel inevitable. Like Onoabhagbe, Armsworth had attended the Premier League Pre-Season Camp. And, like Onoabhagbe, he decided to drop down to non-league level for the 2019-20 season, just to play. He signed for Slough Town of the National League South. Finally, somebody wanted him. He'd impressed in a handful of friendlies, earning a modest part-time contract. When the season started, however, he was on the fringes of the team. After just one appearance, as a substitute, the manager told him he wasn't going to get much game time and that he should find another club.

'That was quite difficult to hear,' Armsworth says. 'That was step two in [non-league] men's football, and I ended up playing at step five [with Basingstoke Town], just to get some game time.'

Against mounting odds, Arsmworth still harboured hopes of a professional career in football. At non-league level, though, he found the training routines to be disorganised and unserious. His team-mates would stagger in, still feeling the effects of a heavy drinking session the previous night.

'That was when I realised, "Oh my God, what am I doing here? I've gone from professional youth football to semi-professional at the lowest level, near enough,"' he says. 'But it made me happy that I was finally playing again. I knew that I had to work my way back up as quickly as I could, to get playing at a good level again.'

The season after releasing him, Fulham invited Armsworth back to their academy site to work towards a UEFA B Licence coaching qualification. Having started coaching with Basingstoke, he was grateful of the opportunity to pursue a high-level badge, seeing a new avenue for a career in the game if his hopes of landing a professional deal at Football League level were to fade. But he found it difficult to return to the scene of the first of his high stack of setbacks. 'There were a lot of people asking how the trials were going and things like that,' he says, 'but not many asking, "How are you feeling?" That is the question you want to be asked. That makes you feel like you've actually got someone who cares about you and wants to help, rather than someone who just wants to ask about football.

'They try to make it as known as possible that there are people there to support you. But they don't check up on you themselves. They give you all these numbers. They're waiting for you to contact them. In reality, that is what it's all about.'

A summer had passed between his last day of training with Fulham and his return to the club to study coaching. It had felt like a bleak lifetime. He had suffered disappointment heaped upon more disappointment. He understood how the weight of it all could crush a person. The help and care of the few people who maintained contact meant a lot to Armsworth, but he found the structures and systems of football that profess to protect its vulnerable youngsters to be little more than lip service to aftercare.

'If you don't have the positive attitude of being able to deal with it,' he suggests, 'it honestly is a tormenting period. I'm quite lucky that I wasn't more affected by it than I was. It is a really difficult period. It's been one of the hardest periods of my life. I hate to think what some of the other lads have been through.

'If they are going to be there to support, they have to take responsibility and live up to it.'

***

The players are asked to register on arrival. They are then spilt into teams, introduced to their designated coach for the day and given a kit. They might recognise a face or two as opponents they've encountered over the years, but there is no on-field familiarity with their temporary team-mates, no chemistry. Many players will be forced to play out of position just to get playing time in front of the scouts, typically given three thirty-minute games in which to impress, to salvage hope.

Every season, around 650 boys are offered scholarships with Football League clubs. For the many who don't make the grade, the EFL runs three 'exit trials' each year, attended by upwards of 150 players aged fifteen and sixteen. 'We recognise that a cut-off for a lot of players is when they start scholarships, after the under-16 season,' explains David Wetherall, the EFL's director of youth development. 'That's a point where a lot of players are not taken on by the clubs. We run assessment trials for players. They're quite big events. We run them typically quite early in the year, just as their under-16 season is coming to an end, just so the players have the opportunity to impress other clubs, and for the clubs to spot potential talent. One of the roles that plays is not just for the lads who end up getting a scholarship elsewhere but also for the ones who don't, just to have that reassurance that they've tried everything, that they've given it all they've got. Maybe then when other clubs have seen them and they've still not got a scholarship, maybe it's right that they do look for the next period.

'They're available to anyone who's held an under-16 registration at a club in that season. We have three trials, and some lads attend more than one event. They're sizeable operations. It's difficult, because there is obviously a lot of pressure on the lads on those days, but we try to make it as relaxed an environment as we can as a league and try to get the lads to come along and enjoy themselves. A lot of clubs attend. There's also different educational establishments, National League clubs, etc. There's a range of possible positive outcomes for players from these events.'

Typically staged at a small, non-league or EFL ground, or on the ample sports facilities of Loughborough University, the exit trials represent one last, desperate shot at rescuing a future in the game for many of the boys in attendance. More than 100 scouts from Premier League, EFL and non-league clubs assemble in the stands, among pockets of parents. The event has been likened to a cattle market. The teenagers are paraded, and the best are plucked for a shot at redemption. Only a handful will be taken on by professional clubs. Some might be offered a trial with a non-league side. Further disappointment awaits the rest.

For more than ten years, League Football Education (LFE) – the organisation responsible for overseeing the education and welfare offerings within EFL academies – utilised funding provided by the EU's Erasmus+ scheme to organise placements with professional clubs in Sweden for dozens of teenagers released by English academies. This was another possible avenue to an extended stay in the game for the boys on show in the exit trials. But the news in early 2021 that the UK government had declined the EU's offer of extended Erasmus eligibility for British youngsters post-Brexit means an almost certain end to the LFE's Swedish Player Placement Programme. Another door closed.

More than 250 players attended EFL exit trials in 2017. Of those, seventy received some form of an expression of interest from the watchful scouts. Around one in nine were ultimately offered a scholarship contract.

'It's a bit of a strange experience,' says Marvin Sordell, the former England under-21 striker who attended the EFL exit trials after being released by Fulham in 2007. 'Your name is on a list with ten other strangers, to play some football, play a game. There are tons of scouts there. You're sat in a changing room with all these guys you don't know. You know that you're about to walk out and your dreams are on the line with how you perform.

'You see a lot of the other boys there are very nervous, very anxious. I'm lucky, because in those circumstances I usually thrive. For some reason or another, I usually thrive in an environment where it's that much pressure that it's literally make or break. Fortunately for me, I was able to get scouted for Watford, amongst a host of other clubs, and that was that. It is a high-pressure environment. It is just parents and scouts. There are tons of scouts standing there, watching, making notes. You think every moment matters when you're on the pitch and you're not playing a full match. That's it. That's what your dreams lie on.'

It is prohibited for the scouts to contact players and parents on the day of the trials, but Sordell says more than one pushed their card into his mother's hand in the stands. In the days after the event, each player is sent a letter through the post informing them, like a football equivalent of speed dating, of which clubs, if any, are interested in seeing more.

'I remember my mum had spoken to a scout a few months before,' Sordell says, 'and he had said, "If you get the opportunity to go to the exit trials, go to all of them, because it gives you more of an opportunity to put yourself in front of people." That was that. The club said, "Would you want to go to the exit trials?" To which I said yes. They asked which ones. I said, "I want to go to all of them."

'I was pretty much expecting what was going to come at Fulham. I was prepared to fight it out, go on trial, see what was to come, whereas there would have been a lot of boys for whom [being released] would have been a big shock. That can be a massive blow. If you've been at a club ten years, eight years, six years at that point, then suddenly you're not, it can be hard to recover, in terms of your confidence and everything. I can only imagine how difficult it is for some. I was lucky, firstly because I wasn't at the club that long, and secondly, I knew I wasn't going to get my scholarship, so I was mentally prepared. If you're not and it comes as a big shock, to be able to pick yourself back up and go and perform to save your dream is very, very difficult.'

Paul Mitten, a former Manchester United apprentice, believes released players' preparedness for trials is one of the most misunderstood and overlooked factors in the post-academy recovery process. In his work as a personal trainer, several young men released by top-level academies in the north-west in recent years have sought his expertise to help them get back to peak fitness but also help them absorb and recover from the psychological impact of the rejection they've suffered. 'What I am passionate about is that the lads who get released, they need to be surrounded by like-minded people,' he says.

Mitten understands exactly what these players are going through, because he's been there himself. As a small but technically gifted striker, he had trained with Manchester United, the club his family supported, since the age of ten and signed schoolboy forms at fourteen. At sixteen, he was considered one of the best prospects in the region, but he found the wings of his ambition clipped simply by the fact he was, as he puts it, 'unfortunately' part of the Class of '93, the bridesmaid generation to the previous year's Youth Cup-winning crop of David Beckham, Ryan Giggs, Nicky Butt and the Nevilles. 'I was always going to struggle, because every lad from the Class of '92 got a year's pro, so they were never going to sign many from my year.'

As an apprentice, he suffered a torn cruciate knee ligament, keeping him out for the best part of a year. Soon after his return, an

Achilles injury required surgery. He began to suffer performance anxiety, too. Eric Harrison, the revered coach credited with the development of so many of United's homegrown superstars, was a hard-nosed taskmaster. 'Eric was fierce,' Mitten admits, 'and I couldn't deal with him.' Harrison would issue stern bollockings whenever Mitten tried any form of elaborate move, so Mitten stopped trying. He kept things simple, and simple isn't enough to earn a professional contract with Manchester United.

After being let go by United – bluntly so; told to clear his locker, say his goodbyes and leave – Mitten climbed aboard the trial merry-go-round. He had try-outs with Bury, Stockport County, Crewe, Nottingham Forest, Tottenham. 'I made a shocking decision,' he says. 'When I left United, my first club on trial was Bury. They trained at Lower Gigg Lane, and it was worse than Gigg Lane. I'm only five-eight, and I played up front. They launched it, and I just got smashed for a week. They let me go at the end of the week. Within ten days, I'm not good enough for United and now I'm not good enough for Bury. It's the initial decisions that are so important.'

Mitten eventually earned a two-year contract with Coventry City, on £175 a week. 'I wasn't bothered,' he says about the measly wages he was offered by the then-Premier League club. 'I couldn't believe I'd got back in the game.' But, once again, rejection was waiting just around the corner. After a handful of reserve games for Coventry, he tore his cruciate ligament a second time. He fought his way back to fitness, only for the club to hand him a gut-punching indignity during pre-season.

'They put the squad numbers up at the start of the season,' Mitten remembers. 'They went one to twenty-seven, then from twenty-seven to forty was blank, but my name was number forty. The lads were looking at me, like, "What's that about?" You feel sick. All the pros upstairs were getting measured for club suits. You're a pro; you go up. "There isn't one for you." It just rips your guts out. Brutal. Two little things like that. It's savage. Really tough.

'I'll never forget, Gordon Strachan was in charge. He told me I was getting released. It was the same again: downstairs, black bag, get your boots – "Lads, I'm off." Back to your digs; get your gear. I drove back up to Manchester. That was it. Done.

'Then I just went down. I got worse and worse. I played for Southport in the Conference, Stalybridge Celtic. You just drop down the leagues. And the lower I went, the worse I got, to the point I just jacked it. I had a season at FC United when they started, because my mate got the manager's job. But you just end up hating it.'

Mitten was twenty when he was released by Coventry. He says he was thirty-five before he felt as though he had fully recovered from the psychological pounding football had dealt him. 'I was a massive red as a kid,' he says. 'My granddad [Charlie Mitten] was very successful at United. I was a massive red. Then you despised them and hated them, and they won everything for twenty years, with lads you grew up with. And you're thinking, "He's not that much better than me." At sixteen, I was in the top forty in the country. Two years later, I was struggling to pass it ten yards.

'That's there,' he says, as he taps his temple. 'You've still got that ability, but it's all those little life events and the way you've been coached, mentally how you perceive yourself – "I'm not good enough. I'm not good enough." At the end, the release by Coventry was probably a relief.

'I say to these lads now, "Do you like football?" And they're like . . . [shrugs]. You used to run home from school, get changed, go out on the field and kick a ball around for free. But getting paid brings pressure. It's performance anxiety. I bet if you asked any of them, "Hand on heart, do you like football anymore?" they don't like it, or they can't cope with the pressure it brings. But that should be avoidable if you manage them the right way.'

Mitten's day-to-day work as a personal trainer – his qualification for which was funded by the PFA – is conducted out of a gym in Stockport. Due to his location and his history in the game, footballers released by the area's professional clubs – particularly Manchester United and City – began to contact him in 2016, looking simply for specialised fitness work to get them back into playing shape. But Mitten applied his own experience in football and utilised the Astroturf pitch connected to the gym in which he rents space to offer a more comprehensive package. He'd draw up a conditioning plan for the young players, but he'd also put on technical sessions on the pitch and sit them down to offer advice and a sympathetic ear.

'Devonte Redmond just broke down,' Mitten says of the former United academy midfielder he helped prepare for a trial with Salford City. 'I sat him in the office and told him what I went through, and I said, "This is happening to you, isn't it?" He said, "Yeah," and he started crying. I said, "Let it out. Don't tell me you don't cry yourself to sleep at night." He said, "Yeah." I said, "You're not nuts. You're not mentally ill. You're normal. But you're not going anywhere until I've got you fit."

'The phone stops ringing. Agents don't want to know them. Their mates stop ringing. They become very lonely. They don't know what to do. So Dev, out of his own pocket, he trained with me three times a week for six weeks. I pushed him hard and he worked great. And then an agent contact I know said he can get him in at Salford. He did great, but he's made bad decisions since then.

'Gribbo [Callum Gribbin], who came to me, he signed a four-year deal at Man United when he was seventeen. They gave him fortunes. I've never seen anyone do such things with a ball. He's got a wand of a left foot. But he's a complex guy. Mentally, he's a complex character. He's at Barrow now, with David Dunn. He's been on the bench a few times but I don't know if he's had a kick.'

After four years of working closely with young, down-on-their-luck footballers, Mitten decided to formalise the care and recovery offering he had devised. In the early months of 2020, he set up Revive, his company through which he provides a rehab-like programme to catch the young men spat out by the academy machine.

'It came through organically,' he explains. 'More lads started coming to me. Lads who were still in the game. Big Ro-Shaun Williams, who's at Shrewsbury, came to me in international breaks and the close season. You end up being a mentor for them. You get their respect. Then I thought, "I want to do this properly."

'I've always stressed, "You're not always going to get back into football, because some of you just aren't good enough. But what I can do is get you in the best physical and mental condition for the rest of your life. I'll help you accept it and how you come to terms with the acceptance if it's not football. I've got partners I work with who can help you with employment or education."

'I had success doing it on a one-to-one basis. Now I'd love to do it with every lad in the north-west, eighteen to twenty-two, who gets released. A lot of them get other clubs straight away, which is great. But the ones who don't, they can come to Revive.'

It has always grated on Mitten that the players who come to him have had to fund the rehab work themselves. Many of them never reached a level of the game where they'd earn vast sums of money. They are investing in the faint hope of reigniting their football careers. Mitten feels the work they require, the service he offers, should fall under the duty of care clubs owe their cast-offs. He has made several attempts to foster a working relationship with clubs and governing bodies, but so far to no avail.

'For one, it was annoying me that lads had to pay for it themselves,' he says. 'Not the lads still at clubs; I admire their attitudes, because I always say you have to differentiate yourself. When the full-time lads come in, that's fine, they've got to pay me my hourly rate for a session. But for the lads who are struggling for money, more care is needed here. These clubs, big clubs, have got a duty of care. I put Revive together. I started doing some planning, some fitness, running, sprint drills, and can do the football coaching as well, all at my facility. I put this programme together. I thought, "I want to take this to the clubs." And they've not bit.

'These lads were coming to me and they were paying me my hourly rate out of their own pocket, and it's not cheap. Some of them were coming three times a week, and I thought, "They shouldn't be paying for this." A few of the lads had been on good money at City and United in their early twenties, so it's fine for them. But some of the lads, I'm thinking, "They're really struggling." They should be released with a transition fund. Don't give it to the lad, so they can gamble it, drink it, snort it. It goes to us. They need day-to-day interaction. They need two to three hours a day with strength and conditioning, a football technical session or a running session, then you have to mentor them at night, because the phone never stops WhatsApp-ing – constant. I think they need ten to twelve hours a week, pretty much like they had at the club, but it's with a different approach in order to get it right.

'Someone at United said they're looking at [running a similar programme at] Carrington. Great you're looking to do it, but that's the last place you should do it. That place is a bad place for them. It has to be at a place away from that badness, where it's a positive environment, surrounded by like-minded people. But it needs funding, and that's the issue we've got at the moment.

'I had a meeting with City about nine months ago. I sat in the canteen – sat for ages. And these two women from the welfare team sat down. I said, "Have you seen my website?"

"No." I was sat with the wrong people, really. They didn't really get it from a football point of view. They said to me, "Every player we release gets a club." "OK," I said, "the percentage will be high, because you're Manchester City and you recruit better players. But when you say 'gets a club', do you mean a contract or a trial? Because your job isn't done if you think, 'Oh, they're going to Rochdale on Monday.' That's not your job done." Nine times out of ten, at the end of that two-week period, they'll get released by Rochdale, through various reasons. One, they're not fit enough to go anywhere. Two, they're not playing enough football, because they've been released they tend to have not played many minutes; their touch is out, their timing is out. The biggest one is they're not prepared mentally. You're going from Disneyland – which is the Etihad Campus, where all your kit is laid out for you every morning and they ask you what you want for lunch, and the pitches are perfect, the balls are perfect and you play lovely little stuff – to a very, very different situation.'

Mitten's long-term vision for Revive involves a bespoke facility somewhere in the north-west, a place released players can go, away from the scene of their heartbreak, and rebuild. Ideally, he'd like to then see franchised centres dotted around the country, catering for all of football's lost youth. This would first require the closed-off world of football academies and youth-development governance to embrace the help he and others like him can offer.

'Everyone is saying more needs to be done,' Mitten says, exasperated. 'Every article ends with "more needs to be done." I can offer you the solution, because I know what it is. Let's identify what's gone on early on, see what help they need. That's how Revive came about. But I've had no joy with anyone. The PFA see us as a threat. They offer courses but it's stuff the lads have got to go out and ask for. But there's an ego, isn't there?

They don't want to go and ask for help, even though deep down they probably do.

'I said to City, "One day, a lad is going to leave here and take his own life." And they looked at me like I had two heads.'

David Wetherall is right to suggest there is more support on offer now for released players than there was when Mitten was cut loose by United in the 1990s. 'There's been a massive increase in this duty of care area,' he says. Manchester City, for example, say a member of their five-person welfare team contacts released players once a month for six months, and the club offer capped funding for psychological counselling. Wolverhampton Wanderers employ four psychologists to work with players released from their Category One academy, and a recruitment team commits to working for up to six months to find a new club for each player. In the Football League, the LFE runs welfare programmes, and the EFL say they track released players for up to three years. 'A big part of what's happened in the game over the last few years is about preparing players for life away from football,' Wetherall continues. 'There was a review of duty of care that Baroness Tanni Grey-Thompson ran in 2017, and we looked at the headings from that, in terms of the personal development, life skills, in terms of the transition and exit strategies. It's a requirement now that each club has these in place; they're core aspects of the academy system.

'One aspect of this is preparation for when they leave football, because people will at some point in time leave football, be it when they're thirteen or when they're forty-three. We have requirements within the system to try and help prepare players, so they're not just, "I'm a footballer . . ." The education side has a big focus on personal development and life-skills programmes, which cover a wide range of subject matters but are a core part of every academy's delivery. And making sure that every club has an induction and also a transition strategy or an exit strategy for when players leave. They've also got a transition officer who tracks the scholars for three years after they leave, which is a point of contact who can identify a need for support. There is a lot going on.

'I think there is a lot of good work in this area, about the strategies when players leave, and it has been an area where I think things have improved, finding opportunities for players when they leave. We'd be naïve to think it's perfect in every scenario, that's not what I'm saying, but it's certainly an area where things have improved, and hopefully things will continue to move in that direction.'

But for all the work that has been done to improve the welfare offering within the academy system, football's clubs and governing bodies seem to believe they are closer to providing full and adequate aftercare than the lived experiences of many released players would suggest. ITV News conducted a survey of young players released by clubs in England's top four divisions during the 2019-20 season. Of the more than 100 respondents, seventy-two per cent felt they were not given enough support by the club that released them, and eighty-eight per cent reported feeling anxious or depressed since being released.

The Elite Player Performance Plan stipulates that clubs must employ welfare officers and have protocols in place to support players in the aftermath of release. The EPPP audit process checks only that these measures exist within each club, though; the efficacy of the protocols is not scrutinised. 'What point are policy and procedures if they don't work in practice?' asks Pete Lowe of Players Net, the independent advice service for young players and their parents. 'I believe football is a very reactive business. It's not proactive. A lot of players are now speaking up about depression and mental health. I have been told that this year, in 2020, the Sporting Chance Clinic has received 1,400 requests for help from players.

'One of the biggest pressures is when players are released from football clubs. The football clubs would turn around and say, "Well, we do everything for the player before we release him and after we've released him." It's a huge issue. We dealt with the case of a player who spent twelve years at a football club and was released in a car park by the academy manager, who told him, "You're not needed any more. Go and clear out your locker." That's horrendous. No warning. No build-up. No easing in to the process.'

Just months after Mitten met with Manchester City and cautioned that the day would come when a released player takes their own life, his prophecy, tragically, came true.

Jeremy Wisten joined City at the under-13 level and was a talented and well-liked member of the club's academy during his time there. He later began to struggle with injuries, and in 2018, shortly after he'd turned sixteen, he was informed that he was not going to be offered a scholarship contract. 'He went for trials elsewhere, but because he hadn't played much football it proved very difficult,' his parents said in a statement following his suicide in 2020 at the age of eighteen. 'We helped him look after himself and encouraged him to take up other sports to keep himself fit until he left us.'

'He suffered while he was at City and after he left there,' Wisten's father, Manila, later told the *Sunday Times*. 'I want to highlight the issue that kids in football need to be taken care of mentally.'

Wisten, unfortunately, is not the only example of the potentially tragic effect of the death of the football dream, of maladjusted youngsters shepherded out from the cushy academy confines and into a harsh reality. Reece Staples, released by Nottingham Forest in 2009, turned to small-time drug smuggling when unable to find a route back into the game. Just months after his Forest rejection, he swallowed nineteen packets of cocaine and boarded a flight from Costa Rica to the UK. One of the packets burst in his stomach. He died on the floor of a police cell. He was nineteen years old.

In 2013, Josh Lyons committed suicide, ten years after being rejected by a Premier League club as a sixteen-year-old. At the inquest into his death, it was said he'd been 'a happy and bright and fun child who was a talented footballer' before spiralling after the game he so loved rejected him. 'I find that it was . . . that pivotal point that crushed a young boy, a young man's life and all the dreams that go with it,' the coroner said. 'It is the one, I find, the single most important factor that led to the events which ended [in his suicide]. I think it's very difficult to build up the hopes of a young man and for them to be dashed at a critical age, when a boy becomes a man. To be found wanting in every way, it's very cruel.

'I am not here to pronounce on football clubs that make the arrangements about young footballers and giving them hopes, because they are not here to explain it,' the coroner continued. 'But to have no support for that letting go seems to be adding cruelty upon cruelty. And that lack of support, I find in absentia of the football clubs to be a certain and compelling factor in what happened ultimately, and I find [Lyons] was a statistic of that.'

In a 2015 study, Dr David Blakelock of Teesside University found that fifty-five per cent of players suffered 'clinical levels of psychological distress' within twenty-one days of being released by their club. Blakelock, himself a former youth player with Newcastle United and Nottingham Forest, believes academy players form an 'athletic identity' through their years spent in the system, and that they then suffer 'a loss of self-worth' when that identity is stripped from them.

'I read the lad Jeremy [Wisten] had been on trial at five clubs,' Mitten says, 'but he wasn't fit. He wasn't fit to do himself justice.

Therefore, it's five more kicks in the balls for this young lad who, all his life, City have paid for him to go through the schooling at [St.] Bede's [College, the private school where City send many of their academy players]. There was never, ever anything enter his head of, "I'm not going to make it." It was, "I'm going to be at City." Then it's a rush to stay in the game, which I totally understand. It ends up [that] the hole gets deeper.

'There's a duty of care to look after them. Not forever. Not for the rest of their lives. Just through this transition period. Probably the most crucial are the three to six months when you have to realise that their dream of playing for that football club is never going to happen. I did read somewhere that a psychologist has likened it to the loss of a loved one. That makes sense, because this is probably what they've loved most through all their life, and then it's taken away from them. So through that transition period, they really need a lot of time. And it's not on the phone; it's hands-on. They need to have a purpose.

'Being brutal, [clubs] tick boxes. If you've been released and you haven't heard anything for three months, then a lady on the phone you've never heard of says, "How are you feeling?" You'd say, "Yeah, I'm fine." The initial transition period from getting released to either getting another club or employment or education, that isn't a phone call. That isn't a hotline to ring.'

It is when rejection compounds, when release is followed by knockback after knockback, that these young people most need the care football purports to provide. Disappointment, for most, is inevitable; the tragedy to which it can lead, the extent of the deep and profound heartbreak rendered by the shattering of improbable dreams, is entirely avoidable.

'A lot more support needs to be given to these young lads, because it was a big part of their lives,' says Scott Armsworth. 'If they're not given support, their dreams can be crushed and they fall out of the game.

'You're going on trial after trial and it's, "Sorry, no, you're not good enough." It's a very hard three or four months. Hearing the news, time and time again, that's when the support is important.

'How many times can you face rejection?'

CHAPTER EIGHT

THE PLATINUM PRODUCTION LINE

'GET AT TRENT! Get at Trent!' Neil Critchley bellowed from the side of the pitch as Bobby Adekanye was fed the ball. Seventeen-year-old Trent Alexander-Arnold was new to the role of right-back, a fish out of water. Until now, he'd mostly played in midfield, either wide-right or centrally; he'd even spent some time at centre-back. Right-back brought a whole new gamut of challenges – one-v-one defending, learning how and when to get forward to support the attack, and what exactly to do when faced with wingers faster, stronger and trickier than himself. His head would spin and frustration would build, often to the point he would angrily send balls flying across to the far reaches of the training pitches of Liverpool's academy.

Alexander-Arnold's coaches knew these growing pains were a necessary part of the teenager's adaptation to a new position. The player knew it, too, having bought into the idea of reinventing himself as a right-back. Critchley, who spent seven years coaching in Liverpool's academy – first as under-18s manager, then in charge of the under-23s – before leaving to become

Blackpool's head coach in March 2020, understood that such daily challenges were crucial if Alexander-Arnold was to make steady, incremental gains. Through trial and error – and it was mostly error in those early days – he would learn where best to position himself when an attacker raced toward him with the ball, how to shape his body to influence his opponent's next move, and how to time his challenges so not to overcommit or concede a foul. Critchley would have the best wingers in his squad go up against Alexander-Arnold in training matches. He'd demand they get on the ball as often as possible and run at the fledgling full-back, over and over. In one instance, it would be the dynamic Adekanye; in others, it would be Ben Woodburn or Yan Dhanda.

'If the winger was getting success against him in training, we just used to keep giving him the ball,' Critchley says. 'Some days I'd think, "I've got Trent here; he's going to quit." And the next day he'd come back and it was as if he was like, "Right, I'll show you."

'It was obvious that Trent needed to be confronted and he needed to be challenged. You wouldn't be able to trust him playing in front of 50,000 at Anfield if you knew he was going to quit and give up in the tough moments, which he could do when he was younger. We used to recreate that as best we could. You can never recreate 50,000 people, but you can put him in situations within training where you know he might fail. As long as you let him know the reasons why you're doing it, he can see the reasoning behind it. We did it because we knew he had the potential to go on and be a top player, and we thought that was the best way of helping him. It was tough, but we made it tough for a reason.

'One of his main qualities is him as a person. You only need to hear him speak now at such a young age, he's a very impressive person. He's level-headed, but he has the fire inside him; he hates to lose. When he was younger, he didn't know how to handle those emotions. He used to throw his toys out the pram if things weren't going his way in training. Often, myself or Alex [Inglethorpe, Liverpool's academy manager] would have to say to him, "You need to go and fetch that ball that you've just kicked a mile away," and he'd go off sulking, in a huff, to collect the ball he'd just wellied.'

These moments within training games were carefully designed by Liverpool's coaching staff to stimulate and nurture the precise aspects of Alexander-Arnold's physical, mental, tactical and technical capabilities they'd identified for improvement. A lifelong Liverpool fan who'd been with the club since the age of six, Alexander-Arnold had long been considered one of the academy's standout talents, but such a bespoke development programme and individualised attention to detail was not favouritism in reaction to his immense potential; it is the same for every player within Liverpool's academy.

'Liverpool have a distinct style of play that's come down through the ages, and that's evident even at academy level,' says Liverpool's former under-23s manager Michael Beale, who is now part of Steven Gerrard's coaching staff at Rangers. 'But the plan is to focus on the individual and give them a real platinum service. That's driven from the owners, [director] Mike Gordon, [sporting director] Michael Edwards and Alex Inglethorpe down. That's the philosophy of the club and it's something the club pride themselves on. It might not be unique to Liverpool, but because Liverpool really believe it in, they're stronger than most other clubs in that type of work.'

Inglethorpe joined Liverpool as under-21s manager in 2012, having previously occupied the same role at Tottenham. He was appointed to replace Frank McParland as academy manager in 2014. As well as trimming the club's bloated age-group squads and overseeing the diversification of the young players within the academy to better reflect the city and wider society, Inglethorpe has driven an individual-based approach to player development. In addition to Alexander-Arnold, the fact the likes of Curtis Jones, Rhian Brewster, Ki-Jana Hoever and Neco Williams all became part of Jürgen Klopp's first-team squad is testament to the efficacy of the methodology.

'It was never around the game on a Saturday,' Critchley explains. 'The players in the team were always more important than the team. If you produce better individual players, then the team will improve anyway' – as Liverpool's 2019 FA Youth Cup triumph attests.

When Critchley joined Liverpool in 2013, he was already accustomed to a similar approach to youth development. As a player, he was an apprentice at Crewe. He attained his first coaching qualification at seventeen and began to coach in the club's centre of excellence, as required by Crewe's apprenticeship programme. Critchley continued to coach the club's youngsters even after leaving to pursue playing opportunities in non-league, and he took up a full-time coaching position within Crewe's academy at twenty-seven, once his semi-professional playing career had wound down. There, he found a philosophy similar to Inglethorpe's Liverpool ideal.

'Every decision was made around the players within the academy,' he says. 'If that was your son, what decision would you make? When the players run the academy, if you like, it helps to give you so much clarity. That has to be driven from the top, and I was so fortunate at Crewe to have that. When I went to Liverpool, Alex was very similar to what I'd experienced at Crewe. I found it quite easy, because I always knew what the end goal was and I always knew what we were trying to do. There was no ambiguity, there were no black spots.'

Liverpool's focus on the individual necessitates constant communication, both among staff and between coaches and players. First, the coaches determine the needs of each player, then comes the implementation and review process, communicating and collaborating with the player to ensure total buy-in. As it related to Alexander-Arnold, once it had been determined that a change of position would best suit his development, Inglethorpe and Critchley, his under-18s manager at the time, sat him down in one of the small offices on the academy complex. They talked him through their plan, discussing its benefits and using videos to help him visualise how his game was to evolve.

'Some of the best coaching goes on off the pitch, in the office, speaking with the players and getting to know them as people,' Critchley explains. 'The plan is always better if it's a joined-up plan and the player believes in it as well. If Trent thought he couldn't play right-back or he wanted to be a midfield player, then it never would have worked.

'We used to conduct regular reviews with the players. I remember doing quite a few with Trent, sitting down with him and taking him through areas of improvement. When he plays at right-back, he's got a range of technical attributes and the way he sees the game. He'll pass the ball like a midfielder from right-back because he used to play in midfield. We thought that was going to be his position because we thought he was better when he saw the game in front of him. At right-back, you're always moving forward, coming on to the ball. That was something we spoke long about. Many different opinions were shared – sometimes agreed, sometimes disagreed. In the end, it worked out well for him.

'He was receptive to the work that we were planning to do with him. Sometimes it appeared maybe he wasn't, because sometimes you'd think, "Is he taking it in? Does he really believe it?" But then, on another day, he would prove you wrong.

'Because he was level-headed, he took things in his stride – that's one of his best qualities. Sometimes Alex would use counters on his board with pictures of the players' faces, to say, "Look, at this moment in time, you've got all these players ahead of you. If you play here, it will give you the best opportunity." But we wouldn't just be moving players because we thought it would be a quicker way to the first team. We'd only be doing that if we thought it was right for the boy, if we thought it would give him the best opportunity to progress.'

With such a grand undertaking as the one the Liverpool coaches were asking of Alexander-Arnold, Critchley found he had to be adaptable and malleable in how he provided coach-to-player feedback. He had to be receptive to the player's mood and cognisant of not flooding him with too much information at once for fear of disillusioning him to the task.

'It's all around the context and the timing,' he says. 'It's the words and how you talk. Sometimes it was friendly conversations; sometimes it was brutal honesty; sometimes the players didn't necessarily like hearing what you were saying, but if they always knew it was coming from the right place, they could accept it.

'It was an ongoing process. It's the level of support that you give. That comes down, for me, to the coach's experience, his intuition, his eye. It's a feeling. Sometimes you think, "No, I've said enough this week. I don't need to speak to him now. I need to leave him alone, give him some headspace." Sometimes you might think, "I need to tell him now." That comes down to a feeling, that experience of being on the grass and being in that environment for so many years.'

For all the potential Inglethorpe, Critchley, Beale and everyone else who came in contact with Alexander-Arnold saw in him as he progressed though Liverpool's academy, none, surely, could have predicted just how rapidly he'd rise to the summit of the game. By the age of twenty-one, he was an England regular, a Champions League and Premier League winner and arguably the best in the world in a position that, just four years earlier, was alien to him.

It is difficult to comprehend the burden of expectation the young man has carried, too. Every football club is representative of its people and its community, but few, if any, have such deep-rooted social and political ties to a place and populous as Liverpool Football Club does with the city of Liverpool.

'It's just an incredible place,' Critchley says. 'It grips hold of your heart. Without sounding too romanticised about it, there's just something unique about the club and the people there. It's more than a football club. I know that's a bit of a cliché but it's true. The connection that they have with the people and the area, it goes beyond the game of football.'

That connection, coupled with a thirty-year yearning for a top-flight league title, meant there was a unique pressure on a local, homegrown player breaking into the first team at the time Alexander-Arnold did in 2017. As a devoted fan, he had watched as his idol, Steven Gerrard, and others entertained and inspired in front of the Kop while always falling agonisingly short of the ultimate aim, that elusive title. Where his heroes failed, Alexander-Arnold succeeded in 2020, starring for Klopp's Premier League champions. Getting there was his own glory, but the patience and support of those in the background certainly played a part.

'It wasn't all plain sailing for Trent when he went up to [first-team training ground] Melwood initially,' Critchley says. 'What he had was a very supportive manager who gave him time and opportunity and showed belief in him. That's massive. Trent had a couple of games early on in Liverpool's first team where, by his own admission, he'd liked to have done better, but he was given time and that level of support. His belief grew and his confidence grew, and that's why he is where he is now.'

Liverpool's commitment to prioritising the individual over the collective does not mean they take a cavalier approach to results at youth level – any team selected is expected to be competitive in each match. But winning must never come at the expense of a player's development. This is why Jones and Hoever, who were eligible to play, were not drafted into the Youth Cup final squad to face Manchester City in 2019. Their presence would have increased the Reds' chances of victory, but the duo's continued exposure to first-team training was deemed of far greater importance.

Theoretically, there will be times when one high-potential youngster will be selected to start ahead of a team-mate whose advanced physical and tactical development might make them a safer pick in respect of winning a game, but who is not, in the long run, considered as bright a prospect. Likewise, if a player is struggling in a match, they might be left on rather than substituted, potentially to the detriment of the team's chances of winning, in order to allow the individual to work through the challenge and develop their problem-solving skills. 'It might be what he needs in terms of his development,' says Tim Jenkins, Liverpool's head of development analysis and under-23s assistant coach. 'You might take a hit on that team's performance because of that, but the bigger picture is that you're giving them the experience they need at that time in order to push them. We've still been able to be really competitive. It's just that winning leagues or winning trophies doesn't come before the needs of the players.

'I used to run an academy through a college. From an educational background, you were doing a lot of work around learning plans for the students. It morphed then into, if we're having a parents' evening or some sort of feedback around their education, what can we feed back about their football, and what sort of plans can we put in place for the individuals? When I got here and started to work with Alex, although we didn't know each other previously, we were similar around that. And that kind of idea is fostered and developed since we've both been around the academy. Over that period of time, we've been able to implement that way of thinking and have some development time to try and refine it.'

Jenkins, who joined Liverpool's academy staff from Manchester City in 2012, leads a three-man team of analysts who collate and evaluate match data and video. 'Rather than preparing a debrief for the team about how a game has gone and the tactical report from that game,' he explains, 'our work post-match is more centred around the individuals in the team and how they performed, breaking that down in terms of their position and the things that would link into how we want them to play the game as individuals.

'We monitor that over a period of time to bring together some trend analysis that we can then present back to the players and work with the players so we can get to the point where we might be able to highlight something that's reoccurred over a number of games. Then we can put together a training programme to focus on that element in training. It's highlighting areas of focus that can then be developed on the training field.'

When it comes to the practicalities of Liverpool's individual approach to moulding and improving their youngsters, it can be misconceived as meaning each player works one-on-one with a coach, separate from his colleagues. While this can be the case if a specific technical concern is being addressed, the day-to-day application of the philosophy is much more inclusive and holistic. 'You're incorporating that individual work into team sessions,' Jenkins says. 'It could be something tactical you want to work on, or a particular sort of run, but you need the context of a real game for it to become a realistic practice. Or something around decision-making that a player would need to be in a match-type context to work on. It can't be isolated; it would need to be in the sessions.

'You can think of it as a solely technical thing, but it's not always about that. It's not always about improving their weak foot or their heading. It might be around mentality – do they quit in training sessions? Can we put them under a bit more pressure? Can they be more of a leader? It's quite holistic in terms of how we try and do it. It's not just the technical elements we use and focus on with an individual. It might be something around mentality or fitness.'

The attention Liverpool pay to the specific needs of each player has, in some cases, aided their recruitment, too. 'They had a vision for Rhian,' says Brewster's father, Ian, of the gifted striker's decision to leave Chelsea at fourteen and move to Liverpool. 'I could not believe the depth they went to, and how long they'd been watching him. And everything they said has come to the fore. Other teams offered more money, but it wasn't about that; it was about football.'

In 2018, when Borussia Mönchengladbach offered Brewster the chance to follow the Bundesliga path furrowed by England youth team-mate Jadon Sancho – an approach which so angered Liverpool that they cancelled a proposed friendly with the German side – he felt a sense of loyalty to Liverpool. Brewster rejected the offer and instead signed his first professional contract with the Reds. 'He hasn't forgotten how Liverpool have treated him,' his father says.

Further shaping the club's drive toward bespoke development programmes, past Anfield heroes are regularly drafted in to help refine Liverpool's future stars, providing a rich source of expertise and inspiration. Working either one-on-one or with small groups of players of similar style or position, legendary names from Liverpool's history put on clinics at the academy, from Robbie Fowler passing on his mastery of the art of finishing to Steve McManaman offering invaluable dribbling advice. 'When I was taking the under-23s, that was a common practice at Liverpool,' Beale says. 'You'd have Steve McManaman, Robbie Fowler, Michael Owen coming in from time to time. Steven Gerrard has been back in, and Kenny Dalglish.'

When Pepijn Lijnders was hired from Portuguese club Porto to be Liverpool's first-team development coach in 2015, the highly respected Dutchman introduced the concept of the Talent Group, an initiative he had success with in his previous role. Its aim is to ease and facilitate the eventual transition to the first team of the academy's best prospects. The club's top talents from the older age groups train together and benefit from regular exposure to the senior environment, taking part in first-team sessions.

'The pathway is very clear and open at Liverpool to get to train with the first team,' says Beale. 'Liverpool have shown in the last five, six, seven years that the opportunities for young players, compared to some other clubs, have been high. Just in the time that I was taking the under-23s, in three years, we had around eighteen debuts between Brendan Rodgers and Jürgen Klopp.'

The relationship between the academy and the first team, in theory, is smoother still now that the senior side have departed their Melwood training ground to take up residence alongside the academy facility in Kirby. Their new, state-of-the-art training ground opened in 2020. 'For the players to be in touching distance of those world-class players at Liverpool at the moment, it can only be of benefit,' Critchley suggests. 'I know that's not the case at other clubs, because sometimes you can be on the same site but a million miles away from each other – it all comes down to the people within the building. The manager, Jürgen, has proven that he invests in the young players, he wants to provide opportunities for the young players, and he believes in them.

'That connection will become a lot stronger. Even stronger than it is now.'

***

Around the time Alexander-Arnold was learning the right-back's trade the hard way on the training pitches of Liverpool's academy, twenty miles east, at Manchester United's Aon Training

Complex in Carrington, Greater Manchester, Marcus Rashford was beginning a reinvention of his own.

The United and England star was only eighteen when he made an electrifying entrance to first-team football in February 2016, scoring twice on his debut, a 5-1 Europa League victory over FC Midtjylland at Old Trafford. And Rashford continued his dream start to senior football with two more goals in his Premier League bow, against Arsenal three days later. Exuding confidence, composure and a clinical touch in front of goal, the teenager emerged as one of the most promising and talked-about strikers in Europe. Yet he had been playing as a centre-forward for less than two years.

Rashford had always been enamoured with the art of dribbling. He would spend hours practising his tricks and revelled in his ability to confound defenders with fleet-footedness and mesmerising skill. He was happiest receiving the ball to feet, as either a winger or a No.10, and trying to dribble around anyone who stood in his way.

'At sixteen, we changed him into more of a striker, running in behind,' says Paul McGuinness, who spent two decades as a high-ranking coach in United's youth set-up. In that time, he saw eighty-six academy graduates make senior debuts and twenty-three become full internationals. 'That's a new concept to learn: to not go to the ball, to stay away from the ball and prepare your space and play a little bit of cat and mouse with your defender. He took to that and he was very mature in studying and listening.

'He also had to understand that we didn't push him into the reserves at that time, because that would have been a tougher challenge against bigger opponents. While you're learning a new concept, sometimes it's better to be in an environment where you're more comfortable and get success. But he understood that. It meant he had more time to work on the things we wanted to work on. Those experiences have helped him. But experience isn't just doing these things. You have to reflect on them and learn something from it. He's certainly done that and matured brilliantly, on and off the field.'

The process of identifying and implementing a change of position for Rashford was a result of a methodology remarkably similar to that which saw Alexander-Arnold converted into a right-back at Liverpool. Like their bitter rivals from Merseyside, United also employ an individual-focused approach to developing their young players. 'Marcus was one of the pioneers of that,' says Colin Little, United's under-18s coach. 'He could have gone and played for the under-23s, but we kept him back because he was going to get more chances to learn to finish. It wasn't about winning games of football. It was about making sure Marcus was getting what he needed to develop.

'Michael Owen spoke about it once with me. He was scoring eight or nine goals a game and they could have rushed him up, but he said, "I didn't want to go up and play a level higher, where I might only get one chance in that game. I wanted to practise my finishing." We had already done it with Marcus, but [Owen] told me that had a really big bearing on how he was, because he just wanted to keep scoring goals; he was addicted. Marcus wasn't quite addicted to scoring goals at that moment in time. He was addicted to beating three or four men with step-overs and tricks. We started to build up scoring goals. We put a bit of responsibility on him to say, "You're going to have to score the goals for this team, playing down the middle." Even if he wasn't really keen on it at the time, he started to realise it was important, that the guys at the top level are the ones who make the difference, scoring goals.'

Like Critchley at Liverpool, Little found himself accustomed to how United operate from the moment he joined as under-13s coach in 2013 thanks to his background of having played and coached at Crewe. 'It wasn't just a case of trying to win a game every week to stay in the division,' he remembers of his time at Gresty Road. 'It was, "We're going to keep playing this style of football even if we get relegated, because we're trying to sell players to a higher standard." The coaching was really individualised. They'd see me and say, "You need to be better at this, this and this." All the other coaching that you had at any other club you went to after that was just generic. Crewe's was like being at university. It was really catered to the individual.'

The way this philosophy is put into practice for Little and his under-18s at United follows the same pattern every season. 'You come in on the first of July,' he says. 'You know quite a lot about the players but not everything. You have a week of training at the club, then you usually go to a training camp abroad. After that, you've got them all day, every day, for ten days. It's full-on, sometimes three or four sessions a day.

'By the time you come back, you've got an idea, among the staff, of what people are good at, what they need to work on and where they need to go with it. An elite programme is put in place for each player. You have the main body of training each week – shape work, how we want to play as a Man United team, what our pressing is going to be like and how we want to defend. And then there's a bespoke individual programme put into all the spare hours of training. We'll make sure we've got the players working on the things we've flagged up they need to work at. You work on that for a few years.

'It's the detail within the detail. You look at the foot patterns they're making to get in position and score a goal. If they are getting it wrong, you go back and look at footage with them – maybe one tiny step to the side, then a side-foot finish. All the little, tiny details, they really buy into that. You can get really big gains from that. On a Monday, I might be working with three or four full-backs; on a Tuesday, I might be working with the forwards, whether it be [Mason] Greenwood or Rashford in the past.

'When they start to bring it out into Youth Cup games, they'll say, "Did you see that? I did that thing we were working on." There becomes that real connection, not just to you as a coach but between you, the club, the player and how they're making progress in the process.

'It's not just about winning the game on a Saturday. At one point, we didn't win in thirteen games while Marcus was playing for us, but we weren't worried about that. We were thinking of each player as an individual. And out of that team, a lot of them are in the first team now. You should always aim to win games, but it's not whether you win them or not that's important. It's the individuals who get through.'

Rashford's personal plan intensified with his change of position at sixteen, but United begin to shape each player's development long before they reach under-18s football. In Rashford's case, it was noted from an early age how his talent and maturity meant he would need to be pushed out of his comfort zone. Ordinarily, United's best prospects are picked out around the age of thirteen and placed into the Manchester United Schoolboy Scholarship programme – referred to as MANUSS for short. MANUSS is a full-time scheme whereby the players are placed in an affiliated school and combine their studies with daily training sessions. Rashford, at age eleven, became the youngest player to join this elite group.

'We took the best players and put them in Ashton-on-Mersey School, and then they would come in training in the day,' McGuinness says. 'They'd mix a bit of extra school work in with coming into the club. That was the important point for him because it gave him extra stability. The big thing about it was the challenge point. He came into it as the youngest person ever in that group. That meant he was challenged all the time

– socially, he's challenged with older players who become like older brothers, but also technically, he's playing with the best players who are older than him.'

By twelve, Rashford began to train sporadically with the under-18s group, which at the time included future first-team colleagues Jesse Lingard and Paul Pogba. He'd join in with small-sided or even one-v-one contests on a small, caged pitch. And when a bout of Osgood-Schlatter disease – a common knee condition among growing adolescents – affected his pace in his mid-teens, he dropped deeper into midfield, refining his playmaking skills. Add in two years of honing his striker's instincts, and by the time of his debut for the senior side at eighteen, Rashford was already a remarkably well-rounded forward, technically and temperamentally.

When it comes to tactical understanding, though, that's one area of their young players' development with which United actively avoid going into too much depth too early. Little, now in his mid-forties, was never part of a centre of excellence in his youth. Instead, he learned the game in the lower leagues. In doing so, he came to understand that the tactical details of any position can be acquired relatively easily and shouldn't be emphasised at the expense of a young player's creativity and self-expression. 'When I used to watch the youth players play, there was a freedom about them,' he remembers of observing United's academy players when he first joined the club. 'They were getting it right. Not too professional too soon, a lot of skill involved, giving them the freedom to be skilful, not too much rigid formations. It was like, let them be themselves and we'll put the other bit in later.

'When you have such talented players, you've got to let them grow into what they want to be. I remember speaking about a player – it might even have been Marcus – and it was, "He should know his job by now." And I said, "Why should he know his job by now?" When you get in the first team, you rarely get in in the position you play anyway. Mason Greenwood is a centre-forward, but at the moment he's playing on the right. Brandon Williams, he's a right-back, but he's been playing left-back in the first team. I've done a bit of research on this. If you're eighteen and you're a centre-half, you usually go in and play right-back, like Jamie Carragher did. If you're a midfielder, you usually get put on the right or the left because they don't trust you in the middle as a young lad. And it's just not that hard to help people positionally in their role.

'I remember someone from the FA saying, "About fourteen, fifteen, you should know where you want to play and really nail down that role in the team." I wasn't too convinced of that. I was a goal-scorer, but I always got played out wide. If a club has a rigid formation and says, "This boy's a right-back," and he stays as a right-back from under-12s all the way to under-18s, I think you've not let him develop into the kind of player he could be.'

In the weeks before Rashford's debut against Midtjylland, stories emerged in the media about how United's academy had been neglected in recent years, falling behind the likes of Liverpool, Chelsea and, in particular, cross-city rivals Manchester City. 'Manchester United's Academy Has Been Reduced to an Underfunded Afterthought' claimed the headline of one *Daily Mail* article; 'Neglected Facilities & 12 Defeats in a Row: Why Man United's Youth Teams are Falling Behind' began a piece on Goal.com. The under-19s had failed to progress from the group stage of the UEFA Youth League; the under-18s had lost twelve games in a row, were bottom of the North Division of the Under-18 Premier League and had been humiliated in the FA Youth Cup, losing 5-1 to Chelsea; and the under-14s had been turned over, 9-0, by City. It was a bleak period for a club with a long and proud tradition of rearing exciting, high-achieving young footballers in-house, the home of the Busby Babes and the Class of '92.

'I was in the academy at the time and I felt it was unfair,' Little contests. 'Were they judging it by the results of the youth teams? Because results aren't important. There are teams that win the Youth Cup and all sorts of other tournaments and never get a player in the first team. It doesn't mean that you don't aim to win the Youth Cup, but don't let it override all the work that's going on.'

United's belief in the process soon proved well-founded. Rashford's lightning-rod debut heralded the arrival of another young star worthy of mention alongside the club's great homegrown products of the past. The following season, Scott McTominay, Axel Tuanzebe and Angel Gomes all made senior debuts, and United topped TrainingGroundGuru.com's Academy Productivity rankings for 2016-17 and 2017-18. In 2019-20, under Ole Gunnar Solskjær, seven academy graduates made ten or more Premier League appearances, with striker Greenwood emerging as yet another superstar in the making.

'There's a scarlet thread of youth development that has been woven through our club down the years,' assistant academy director Tony Whelan says. 'I think it's because we've always valued young people. We've understood young people are special, and that you can grow them within your football club and you can get them into your first team. That was certainly the goal for Sir Matt [Busby] and Jimmy Murphy back in the day. In the gap between Sir Matt retiring and when Sir Alex [Ferguson] arrived in 1986, there was an interregnum, but then [Ferguson] revived it, culminating in the Class of '92 and through to today, with Mason Greenwood and young Brandon Williams getting in the first team.

'There's always been an expectancy at the football club from supporters that youth development will be a priority, because of the Busby Babes, because of what they meant, because of what their lives meant, because they died for a cause. I think it goes back to those days. There's always been a high expectancy for us to produce players of that ilk. That's been indelibly woven into the fabric of the club. It's something that's been handed on and handed down. Can you imagine a Man United team coming down the tunnel and Old Trafford and there's not one player from the youth system in it? It goes back to Sir Matt. There's been this desire and effort and will to see it happen, that that thread isn't broken. It's historic. It's something the people within the football club that have preceded me – people like [youth coaches] Jimmy Ryan, Eric Harrison; before that, Wilf McGuinness, Johnny Aston, Jack Crompton – all of those people shared that same view, that same vision, and they did their bit. And I'm at this end now, and I feel it very, very strongly in my bones.'

In December 2019, United celebrated reaching the milestone of 4,000 consecutive matches in which a graduate of their youth system had featured in their first-team squad. A staunch faith in their methodology might have led to results at youth level, for a while, taking an alarming dip, but the platinum production line never stopped churning.

CHAPTER NINE

A SOUL WORTH SAVING

A MASKED MEMBER of staff walks a constant loop of the indoor training area, a tank of sloshing disinfectant strapped to her back. One after another, she sprays each of the fold-down seats that surround the pitch. When all have been zapped, she begins her round again. Alternating green and red stickers indicate which of the seats can be used, in order to adhere to a policy mandating a two-metre distance between every non-player in the building. On one side of the artificial playing surface, which is bisected and outlined by dozens of two-foot-high rectangular foam blocks, the girls' under-16s team trains; on the other, a handful of prospective physiotherapist hires, faces covered by surgical masks, are being scrutinised. It is the evening after nationwide lockdown measures were eased in the midst of the coronavirus pandemic, and Liverpool's academy is a buzzing hive. Women's academy manager Julie Grundy, ten hours into a twelve-hour working day, is queen bee.

The academy facility is situated at the south end of a 56-acre site shared with the first-team's brand new £50million training complex in Kirkby, seven miles from the centre of the city. Above a set of double doors inside the main building, the words 'We are Liverpool. This Means More' are emblazoned in large red typeface. Lampposts lining the roads that snake around the grounds carry posters of homegrown legends of the club's past; images of Michael Owen and Steve McManaman occupy pride of place in front of the central building's entrance. The giants of history upon whose shoulders Jürgen Klopp's Premier League champions stand, and upon whose success these expensive facilities are founded, are paid due reverence. As she paces the outer perimeter of the academy's indoor pitch, orchestrating arrangements for the interviewee physios and fielding enquiries from colleagues on matters ranging from scheduling to performance to logistics, Grundy allows a brief moment's pause. She reflects on the high-end surroundings to which she and the teams she oversees have daily access. 'This was built by Steven Gerrard, Robbie Fowler, Jamie Carragher,' she says.

As a player, Grundy was the long-time captain of a successful Leeds United Ladies side. She retired aged thirty-four, leaving the field to a standing ovation in the 2006 FA Cup final. Despite defeat to Arsenal, it was a storybook end to a fine career. But, like most of her contemporaries, Grundy's was a playing career fought for against stacked odds. There were no established grassroots female leagues when she was growing up. She was sixteen before she experienced any form of organised football, after a school teacher prompted her to contact Leeds Ladies. She had to work a full-time job throughout her playing career, serving as a girls' football development officer for the West Riding County FA. As reverent as she is of Liverpool's past key figures, Grundy considers it her duty to pay proper homage to the pioneers of female football history. She wants to make sure the new generation are aware of the women who fought for the opportunities from which they now benefit. When a local school invited her to give a talk to their students during the 2019 Women's World Cup, Grundy took the opportunity to impart a history lesson.

'Everyone knew about the Steph Houghtons and all the top players,' she remembers, 'but nobody knew about Gill Coulthard, who is the most capped English player. It was fascinating to see that people don't understand that women's football has been going more than ten years.

'I think it's important that, historically, we still go back to the heritage. There are a lot of females who broke down barriers to now being able to play the game as a pro. I'm always conscious of reminding these [Liverpool players], there were people before you who were ground-breaking, for you to be able to come into this facility and be able to experience this. Even though it's great the game's going where it is, I still think we have to go back and understand what it took to get here and the barriers we had to face.'

Those barriers have been significant and manifold. In the early part of the 20th century, the women's game was flourishing. Matches could attract as many as 50,000 spectators, and by the 1920s there were around 150 women's teams in England. The popularity of female football was to the great displeasure of the game's male-exclusive authorities. In 1902, the FA Council urged men's sides not to play matches against 'lady teams'. In 1921, the stuffy FA hierarchy took their misogyny one step further, prohibiting women from playing on FA-affiliated pitches, claiming football was 'quite unsuitable for females and should not be encouraged'. The ban forced female football underground, preventing women from playing at grounds capable of hosting spectators, stifling any hopes of growth and proper organisation.

It was not until 1971, following UEFA intervention and two years after the formation of the Women's Football Association, that the FA rescinded its ban on female participation. In the fifty years women's football was effectively outlawed, the men's game evolved and grew exponentially; female football has been playing catch-up ever since. Girls' football lagged yet further behind, lacking any of the infrastructure, investment and developmental pathways available to boys. The FA only took full control of, and thus responsibility for, women's and girls' football in 1993, with robust plans for developing elite female players belatedly arriving around the millennium.

Grundy's career was forged in female football's fallow years and culminated with the game in a much healthier state by the mid-2000s. When she began coaching with Leeds United, two years after her retirement, full-time positions in women's football were still rare. She had to juggle multiple other coaching roles to get by. Following an invitation from former England international Sue Smith, Grundy began to coach at the Doncaster Belles, one of England's most famous female teams, having been the subject of a documentary, a book and the inspiration for TV drama in the 1990s. She became manager Neil Redfearn's No2 at Doncaster. When Redfearn left to take charge of Liverpool's women's team in 2018, he asked Grundy to join him and take over as the club's women's academy manager. Here, she feels duty-bound to help elite girls' football continue to grow.

'I love the coaching and managing side of things, but developing the game has always been a passion of mine as well,' she says. 'Where my enthusiasm and passion comes from now is making sure that all the support around that is there. It's now about player care and the education and evolving that support around the player. I like that challenge. For me, that's more rewarding now. I've done the coaching and managing thing for years. The operational side of things is challenging.

'It's a big job, the expectation it brings just by the badge alone. That's something you can never prepare for. It overwhelms you how important in the city this club is. It's a nice overwhelming feeling, that you're working for the biggest football club in the world.'

Liverpool's girls' programme is an FA-licenced Regional Talent Club (RTC), graded Tier One, the highest of the three levels a centre can be assigned. The RTCs are an evolution of the centres of excellence the FA introduced in the early 2000s. The purpose of the centres was to develop players for the national team, as part of an initiative devised and overseen by Hope Powell, England Women's manager at the time – 'She has left a legacy,' Grundy says of Powell. 'We have to remember the work that she's done.'

There were fifty-one centres of excellence around the country, run by clubs and regional FAs that applied for licences and conformed to criteria around facilities and staffing, similar to the model for academies drawn up in the *Charter for Quality* for the boys' game in the late 1990s. However, as one FA insider puts it, 'These weren't centres of excellence. They were centres of pretty bang average,' as a consequence of the sheer number of girls in the centres and the still-growing participation levels in the sport as a whole at the time. These centres typically ran four or five age groups, with perhaps a handful of girls good enough to make the grade in each. The level of expectation placed on each centre was setting many up to fail, too. Each received the same amount of funding, which had to be matched at a minimum, and was expected to produce players at the same rate. Some of the county FAs found this to be a demand impossible to meet, hamstrung, in some cases, by a rural location and thus a shallow talent pool. They were measured against professional clubs with expertise and funding above and beyond what the local authorities could provide their programmes.

In response, the FA decided to reduce the number of licences it would issue, from fifty-one to thirty, and tailor funding and expectations to match the means of each club or authority, and so the RTC programme was born. As before, clubs would have to apply for a licence to run an RTC, only now they would have to apply against the tier system, stipulating the funding they would commit and the productivity of which they expected they would be capable. The target for the RTC programme, broadly speaking, is to produce players to help English clubs win the Champions League, which in turn will raise the standard of players available for England selection, whereas the original centres of excellence were established with the express aim of producing England internationals.

The advent of the RTC model, much like EPPP in the men's game, has increased the amount and quality of training to which girls at higher-tier centres are exposed, driven professionalism levels and created more full-time roles.

'Even with the Doncaster Belles,' Grundy says, 'there was only myself and the general manager [who were full-time]. There were people coming in literally putting their hours in for free because they wanted the club to succeed. That's always been the reliance of the women's game. It's been the gift of people's generosity with their time, but the game can't last on that. We need to make sure that it is professional and it's not reliant on the men's game.'

The FA Girls' Talent Pathway – a plan to map a route from grassroots level to the England senior team for the best young girls – was introduced in 2016. One of the main innovations it has driven is the notion that girls should train and play with boys. While mixed sessions are permitted up until the age of eighteen, many clubs now integrate the sexes to some degree in the younger age groups. Liverpool's girls' under-10s and under-12s teams compete in a local boys' league, a standard practice across RTCs. Grundy, who has fond memories of being 'a bit of a tomboy' playing recreationally among the boys as a child and feeling it helped develop the tough-tackling style for which she became renowned at Leeds, believes mixed-sex play has benefits beyond footballing development.

'The suggestion was to have the under-10s and under-12s play in a boys' league,' she says. 'That was from a developmental point of view, looking at the physical corner and the social corner. There are statistics to show that a female who has come from boys' football or mixed football up to a certain age, rather than a girls' team, in terms of aiding that speed of development, it's factual. And to flip it on its head, it's great for the boys to see that. It kind of normalises it. It's bringing respect into it.'

Arsenal have a long and storied tradition as England's most successful women's team, and their female academy has proven to be equally pioneering in recent years. They are believed to be the first club to use mixed-sex training sessions, and they view their policy of sending their best young female players to train regularly with the boys' academy teams as one of their most potent developmental tools. 'They train in the boys' sessions as normal,' explains James Honeyman, Arsenal's women's academy manager. 'We have three players that do one night a week as an extra night, a couple that do a night instead of our night, because they train on the same night, then we have another one who does two nights with the boys and one with us – she does every Tuesday with us and then alternate Thursdays, just because of where she's at. To be brutally honest, there aren't too many challenges for her in the women's game. She's probably the best youth player I've ever seen, so for her to get her challenges, we need to manage the programme.

'We try to keep them in their own age group as much as possible. But what's great with the academy is you have the flexibility to move them up and down. We've got a couple training down in age group, a couple who train with the right age group, and then we can review at certain points throughout the year.

'I think what would be the great end game would be for a lot of your best girls to be training with the boys, week in, week out. You could have your best five in each age group across the country training at the boys' academy. They've done that in Germany for a very long time, with the boys and girls training together. I think that would be where we want to get to. I think we're ahead of a lot of clubs in terms of girls training with boys.'

For all that mixed-sex matches and training sessions foster a level of acceptance and normalisation around girls' presence in elite-level environments, the extent of the gender inequality within football was exposed by the coronavirus pandemic. When a second national lockdown was mandated in November 2020, football deemed to be of an elite level was allowed to continue. That encompassed the professional game but also Category One boys' academies. All girls' programmes were forced to close their doors.

'That's the women's game's issue,' Grundy says. 'There's still a lot of work to do to bring it up to where people's expectations are. We've seen it evolve and it's been fantastic. It's getting great coverage, with the US players [Christen Press and Tobin Heath] coming over to Man United, for example. But there's still a lot of catching up to do. We're making fantastic strides, but we probably need to be making bigger strides.'

One of the areas within women's youth football most ripe for a raising of standards was highlighted by England forward Nikita Parris. A native of Toxteth, Liverpool, Parris lamented that talented inner-city girls – many of whom are from a BAME (Black, Asian, Minority Ethnic) background – are not being spotted by professional clubs. 'Centres of excellence are not actually situated in areas that are accessible for inner-city communities and the vast majority of BAME athletes or BAME participants are going to come from those areas,' Parris said in October 2020.

The biggest inequality between women's and men's youth football is that of access and opportunity. As Parris noted, few RTCs operate within an achievable commute distance of inner-city areas. Only two London clubs, Arsenal and Chelsea, run RTCs (Tottenham have a girls' programme, but it sits outside of the FA's oversight), and neither is situated within the city: Chelsea's shares a site with the first-team and boys' academy in Cobham, in rural Kent; and Arsenal's is based in St Albans, Hertfordshire, to the north of the city.

Most RTCs operate with next to no recruitment budget. While their male equivalents benefit from worldwide scouting networks and dozens of talent-spotters with eyes trained perpetually on densely populated urban areas, female academies recruit almost exclusively through a trial process. Girls either apply or are invited to attend mass trials at an RTC, and clubs can't – or won't – fund travel in the same way they do for talented boys. Brentford, for example, claim they were spending six figures annually on transporting male players to and from training and games before they closed their academy. Aside from the fact proper talent identification takes the time and effort of multiple viewings, with one-off trials likely to overlook as many players as they find, girls without the means of transport to attend are being missed entirely. 'At the moment, we're selecting talent with our hands behind our backs,' says one FA figure who preferred to remain anonymous. 'Clubs are running programmes that are so hard to access.'

Shortly after Parris's comments, the FA announced its 'Inspiring Positive Change' strategy, a four-year project aimed at increasing access and inclusivity within women's and girls' football. 'We want to ensure there is access and opportunity for every girl and woman to play, coach, spectate, officiate, manage or administer if they so wish and the game to be truly representative of our society across all protected characteristics and social backgrounds,' read an accompanying statement from Baroness Sue Campbell, the FA's director of women's football.

'The challenge around the inner-city girls is women's football is in a place where there is a big burden on parents for travel, there's a big burden on players making their own way to training,' Honeyman says. 'And from the inner-city areas, there aren't too many routes in and out, in terms of being able to get to training grounds. That's the problem. Ninety per cent of the recruitment – maybe ninety-five per cent – in the women's game, they come to us. That's at every club I've ever worked at. We do an open trial, they come to us, and we select.

'Right now, I'd say those [inner-city] kids are being missed. They're being missed because there is no scouting network as such, because there is no scouting budget as such. And also, where do you go and look for these girls? Grassroots girls' football right now is a long way off. That's the challenge. For boys, you've got some very good grassroots leagues. You've got a big infrastructure with there being millions of boys playing every single weekend in certain places. You can go to a venue where there's thirty pitches and watch fifteen games.

'It's not just financial. It's also the infrastructure. For a game to go from a grassroots game to the world-leading women's league, which [the Women's Super League] is now – streets ahead in promotion, in the names and the clubs and everything – the infrastructure is not in place, and we're trying to play catch-up. But when the money comes in, it keeps going into people's first teams, rather than building infrastructures.

'Because the growth in the [women's] game has been so quick, to keep up you've got to keep spending. That means you've got to keep signing players. It has become a bidding war for some players. That means the youth gets left behind because we need to win now. If we don't win now, we can't win in the future. We've got to make the youth player today for tomorrow's game, but we don't actually know what tomorrow's game looks like.'

Some key figures within the women's game believe the logical next stage of female youth development's evolution is to grant yet more power to the clubs, just as the FA's own *Charter for*

Quality recommended in 1997. As the Women's Super League (WSL) continues to grow, there is logic to the belief that youth-development programmes should be attached to its clubs more closely, and that the clubs should have greater autonomy over shaping and integrating their academies.

While Honeyman appreciates the logic of such a proposal, he is not sure the professional women's game, in its entirety at least, is quite ready. 'I think the FA still have a big hand to play,' he says, 'because, at the end of the day, we need to be winning World Cups and we need to be winning Champions Leagues in this country to grow the game. We've got to be winning both. One can't really work without the other.

'I don't know who should control it, but the professional game isn't big enough. There are only twelve teams that are professional. Maybe other teams have gone full-time, but whether they're professional is probably up for debate. Like Leicester, they do brilliant work and they've gone full-time. But are they a professional football club? I'm not sure. That top bracket of professional clubs is probably not enough to control the whole game, with there being thirty academies and twelve teams in the Super League.'

Where Honeyman would like to see a direct mirroring of the mechanics of male youth football is in one of the more controversial aspects of EPPP. The fixed compensation system to which all Premier League and EFL academies are bound has been the cause of great consternation since its introduction in 2012. Many smaller clubs feel it leaves their best young players undervalued and vulnerable to being poached by bigger, richer academies. But in women's youth football, where there is currently no obligation for one club to compensate another when signing a player, Honeyman feels something akin to the EPPP model would be welcome and worthwhile.

'I think a big thing to help this would be compensation in the women's game,' he says. 'Until someone's eighteen, you can't sign them on a professional contract. Someone can walk in Arsenal's training ground tomorrow and say, "We want X. At the end of the season, we'll just sign them for free. You can't stop us." And that means that clubs are reluctant with their investment, because they could invest half a million in a player who then, at the end of the season, just says, "Cheers, I'm going to go and sign for City because my mum lives in Manchester."

'I've been at the other side, where we've made really good players. I remember one year being at MK [Dons] and maybe losing six of our top eight talents to big clubs because they walk out the door to go to a club that could be twenty miles down the road. We felt we couldn't compete and there was nothing we could offer. We got nothing in return. It was just, "Hopefully we'll make another one." EPPP had challenges, but in terms of compensation, it at least meant you were guaranteed something. Even if it undervalued players, it meant that you would get a return on your investment.

'I don't want the game to sell its soul, but if you want people to invest, they have to guarantee they're going to get a return. No one's going to be putting their money on red on the roulette and they don't know what it is going to come out at. They need that sustainability of "even if she leaves tomorrow, we're still going to get £6,000. At least we've got a return. That pays two coaches for a year for us." That's got value to it.'

It's a difficult balance to strike, between ensuring the investment women's youth football needs in order to grow is protected and incentivised, and tempering the creep of commercialism that has besieged the boys' game. Is it possible to pursue growth, to forge opportunities for more careers and a greater degree of professionalism, while also clinging to the purity that still exists in elite girls' football?

'The women's game right now can't sell that big dream to these players, and it shouldn't ever,' Honeyman insists. 'It can't sell the "you're going to be a multi-millionaire at the top of the game."

That doesn't exist. You may, if you are at the very top end of the game, be earning six figures. What makes the women's game currently so pure is that it is just people trying to play the best level they can because they want to play the game.

'If it loses that part of itself and it tries to become too professional, we'll create six clubs that can cope, and then loads of clubs that are nowhere near it. And then the talent will fall through the cracks. And we'll end up with really big hotspots. There'll be a north London one, because we'll stockpile. Chelsea will do the same. Man City will. Man U will do the same. Liverpool will. Maybe Villa. The rest of the country will try and make do. The women's game needs strategic growth.

'At the end of the day, the one thing I've never, ever forgotten in my career is: this is just a game. It's just a really fun game that people love to play. The women's game, that's why I love it so much, because it still is just a game; it's not a multi-billion-pound operation – yet.'

At Liverpool's academy, the under-21s are out on the synthetic, all-weather pitch. The ball pops between flashes of yellow, orange and pink boots. A dense rain swirls around the young women, slicking hair tight against heads. Droplets leap from a nylon net when the ball is lashed into one of the four miniature goals on the boundary of their small-sided game. Grundy pulls up the hood of her grey, club-branded coat before heading out to observe the session.

'I'd like to keep the legacy of the women's game, because it's known as a family game,' she offers as a final thought. 'You go to any game in the WSL, you see the women's players going over to the fans, signing autographs, taking pictures. They're a little bit more connected. There's a family feel. That's what we want to try and keep.'

Just as the Women's Super League's recent emergence and growth echoes the Premier League's early years, borrowing lessons in marketing to the masses, women's youth football is approaching a crucial stage not dissimilar to where its male counterpart previously trudged. A student of history, Grundy is hopeful female football's future remains faithful to its past. She knows there is as much to be learned from the mistakes of the men's game as from its successes. It's OK to sell a dream, just not at the expense of a soul.

***

Although the number fluctuates as roles change and some switch back and forth to the women's game, a head count of the female coaches working in English football's male academies can almost always be tallied on the fingers of one hand. And as Queens Park Rangers' Foundation Phase lead, Manisha Tailor is the only female coach in her position at any professional club.

A shade over four-foot-nine, she stands shoulder to shoulder with many of the eleven-year-old boys she coaches. As a woman in an environment where adolescent players are powered by testosterone and her peers own a Y chromosome – and, as someone of south-Asian descent, where few share her background – Tailor always knew that, in the football world, she was different. She knew that would complicate her ambitions. And she knows that's a problem.

'I grew up in a time when there were not that many girls playing football, and definitely not many women from minority backgrounds,' she says. 'My brother played football, so I just grew up playing football with him.

'I was born in 1980, and it was 1989 before I played in the school team. But we didn't have a girls' team, because there weren't enough girls to build a team, so you're playing mixed football. When I went to secondary school, there wasn't a girls' team. When I spoke to my PE teacher, he said there just weren't enough girls interested. We're going back to '92. Women's and girls' football wasn't as developed as it is now, and there weren't as many pathways, so where would I go?'

'From then, I pretty much thought, "Well, I'm not going to be a player." I didn't know that jobs in coaching existed.'

Instead, Tailor discovered a passion for working with children and began a career in teaching. A knock-on benefit of teaching, she found, was that it enabled her to indulge her love of football by running after-school clubs. She qualified as a teacher in 2001, and by that point her drive to help others, to nurture the potential of youth, had been redoubled by life-changing circumstances.

When he was eighteen, Tailor's twin brother, Mayur, suffered a severe deterioration of his mental health, a result of extreme and prolonged bullying. The trauma of a kidnapping and resultant suicide attempts took him to a place of no return. Their twenty-first birthday was spent at a psychiatric unit, after he had been sectioned. Once inseparable siblings, mutual football obsessives, Mayur couldn't even recognise Manisha.

He has required full-time care ever since; the bulk of which Tailor has juggled alongside her career. He still lives with Tailor and her family, never recovering his ability to speak. She hasn't allowed Mayur's illness and the demands it placed on her to become a barrier, though. She's faced enough of those. Rather, Tailor has been driven by it, her fires stoked by the injustice of what was taken from her brother. 'I don't know what that did but it completely shaped and changed the way I see things,' she says. 'That is my motivator for everything I do. That then became my drive for wanting to fulfil some of the things that he may never get the chance to do, but also using it as a way of navigating some of my frustrations.

'Even outside of football. In education, for example, I completed my trainee headship at thirty-one. That's very young. My first senior leadership role was when I was twenty-two. All I did was work. I became obsessed. And now my drive is: I want to get the players better. I am obsessed with wanting to help the players, wanting to be part of their journey in reaping rewards.'

In 2007, the school at which Tailor was teaching partnered with a coaching outreach programme run by former England international Rachel Yankey. After a discussion with Yankey, Tailor was encouraged to seek formal coaching qualifications, the likes of which she was previously unaware even existed. While obtaining her FA Level 1 and 2 badges, she began to lead weekend sessions at a grassroots club run by Yankey. Four years later, unfortunate family circumstances again intervened to send Tailor's working life in a new direction.

While Tailor was studying for a master's degree in leadership, her mother fell ill, requiring a triple heart bypass. In addition to her duties caring for her brother, she found her daily commute to work to be too taxing. She took a leave of absence from teaching to look after her family and focus on her studies. Just for one school term, she thought. 'As soon as a few people [in football] I was connected with found out I was no longer in education full-time,' she says, '[they] just asked if I'd do bits of work with them, Rachel being one of them.

'I was able to set up my company, Swaggarlicious Limited, which is essentially just me. That allowed me to explore something else. I found a drive and passion for being able to transfer my skillset and experiences into working in football, mainly grassroots football, but looking at the angle of diversity and mental health, particularly through my experiences. I never thought I'd end up working for a football club. Never. That wasn't even on my plan or on the radar.'

Tailor began to give up what little free time she had to coach on a volunteer basis, feeding her passion for the sport but also accumulating tangible experience that, just maybe, could help her pursue a career in the game that had begun to appear faintly possible. An unpaid gig with the Middlesex FA's girls' centre of excellence, in time, led to her becoming centre manager and under-9s head coach. And when the centre shut down, in 2016, she again threw herself into unpaid opportunities in the hope of something more sustainable materialising. At the invitation of Chris Ramsey, QPR's technical director, she began to coach at the London club's academy.

'I volunteered,' Tailor remembers. 'I took a risk. I would spend maybe twenty hours a week there for about four months. I would freelance on all the other days – supply teaching, one-to-one teaching, working with Show Racism the Red Card, delivering different workshops – to get by. I was still doing the volunteering to gain other experiences.

'I took a gamble, really. I worked out how much I needed to earn at the end of each month. I just immersed myself in the nature of the club. Man-marked Chris. If I was allowed to go into meetings, I'd do that. I'd be there at ten in the morning, watching the under-18s. I'd spend time with Paul Furlong, the under-18s coach, Andy Impey and Paul Hall with the under-23s. I'd speak to senior staff. I'd look at the [strength-and-conditioning department], see what they do there. Look at the education. I'd then stay back until the evening and go and watch some of the younger schoolboys and see how things work. It was pretty much just immersing myself and understanding: what is an academy? How is it run? What types of jobs are available in an academy? But more importantly: what does Chris want from a coach? What does the philosophy look like at the club? How can I upskill myself and gain a better understanding of the philosophy?

'Then there were changes in staff. That then opened up for me, four months later, in September 2016, a part-time role with the under-9s. I did that for two seasons, alongside other work. There was an opportunity for me to apply for ECAS, which is the Premier League's coaching mentorship scheme. There is no secret that there was also a big emphasis on black, Asian, minority ethnic candidates and women. But what helped was I was already at the club. They spoke to me and said there are no guarantees, but what it could do is fund a full-time job for me, and would I be interested? I thought that showed a lot of trust and a lot of value in wanting me to be full-time.

'The rest, I guess, is history. I'm into my fifth season with the club, my third as full-time.'

Tailor's drive for self-improvement continues, as she works to add to her UEFA B Licence badge by obtaining her UEFA A Licence, the second-highest coaching qualification in football. She hopes to someday become an academy manager. She is even more determined, though, to help others. Her work raising awareness around mental health issues is unrelenting, and a teaching resource she has authored on the subject has been signed by an education publisher. Through the endeavours of her company, Swaggarlicious, and her work with organisations such as Show Racism the Red Card and Kick It Out, she was awarded an MBE in the 2017 New Year's Honours List, for 'services to football and diversity in sport'.

'The way that we've seen it, it was testament to the journey,' Tailor says of her royal honour. 'My brother's illness has completely changed our lives, the way that we live and the way that we see things. All this frustration I feel, this was a reward to keep going and keep doing the good work in those important areas to help other people. So definitely a testament to the journey, to the heartache and frustrations, which is really nice.

'Also, you look back in history, with the British Empire, especially in India, one of the things I said to my mum was, "There was a time you wouldn't even think that an Indian person would be getting honoured by the Queen." Rather than seeing it in a negative way, it was almost an acknowledgement of: we know what's happened in the past, and it's not about eradicating that, but it's also about not continuing to carry those aggressions. This was about moving on, acknowledging and remembering, and being proud that, in history, would we ever have thought that this would happen? No, we wouldn't have. In that respect, it was important on so many other levels, rather than just the football.'

Tailor's great hope for the game now is that more women and people from BAME backgrounds are given real opportunities. She wants to open the doors that were closed to her at the beginning, to send the ladder back down and elevate those whom football has historically neglected.

'If I can forge a sustainable career in the game, that can help other women like me, or other people from minority backgrounds like me, not just women,' she says. 'In all ninety-two clubs, I'm the only one doing my job. That can't be because you haven't got anybody qualified.

'The ones who have the power to employ, that mindset has to change. Unless that changes, it doesn't matter what initiatives you have. There's all these great initiatives, which I think have a place, but the only reason you have to do that is because there isn't transparency in the processes. If there was transparency, you don't need those initiatives, because you know you're getting treated the same as everybody else.

'If you take me for an example, I'm four foot nine and a half. I'm small. So there is a perception already of me based on my size and my stature. OK, I've been five seasons at the academy now. But I still sometimes feel I'm getting judged on just the way I look. But actually, I'm coming into my fifth season. I'd like to think I know a little bit more now than I did right at the beginning. You're a woman, and you're an Asian woman. Before you even say anything, you're getting judged on those things.'

The real change Tailor hopes to see has not yet occurred. Nor, she fears, is it imminent.

'There's still a lot of sexism,' she says, her exasperation righteous and palpable. 'I think sexism is more of an issue than racism, personally.

'Football has got a long way to go.'

CHAPTER TEN

SYSTEM REBOOT

A LARGE, FIRST-floor meeting room at Burnley's Barnfield Training Centre overlooks eleven full-size pitches. When wintertime sends the rural-Lancashire temperatures plummeting, the outer fields are liable to freeze. The pitch nearest to the reception doors stays a vibrant green, though, pliable and playable all year round, protected from winter's bite by an undersoil heating system. First-team manager Sean Dyche is there, watching on from the sidelines, arms folded, as Nick Pope makes one spectacular save after another. The rain pounds hard against the roofs of the expensive cars packed tight into the car park behind the goal the England keeper defends. The assortment of Range Rovers, Audis and Mercedes are shielded from flying size fives by a twenty-foot-high net. In front of the net there is a small, grey sign. It bears Burnley's crest, encircled by the words 'It's a way of life. Legs. Hearts. Minds.'

Above the scene, sat at the meeting room's wide, rectangular table, academy manager Jon Pepper explains why this way of life has been his target since he was a teenager.

'My ultimate aim was to wear a tracksuit,' he says. 'It sounds really daft. Why would a sixteen-, seventeen-year-old think of that? I wanted to play professional football, so the next-best thing was [coaching]. I lived in my tracksuit, so that's what I wanted to do. I got focused on working in sport.'

That was after any hope of a professional playing career was ended by a severe leg break at sixteen. Pepper's father was club secretary at Stafford Rangers and then Chesterfield, where Dyche was a player. 'All I've known is football,' Pepper says. Turning to coaching, he took a job with Chesterfield's academy when the advent of the *Charter for Quality* created jobs in youth development in the late 1990s. Making a living out of the game that could eventually sustain a family proved difficult, though. He was released after six years managing Bradford City's centre of excellence, and his four years coaching in Nottingham Forest's academy saw him paid only on a session-by-session basis. He supplemented that with a part-time role as head coach of Leeds Metropolitan University, taking over from future Brighton manager Graham Potter, commuting by train several times a week. A move to the United States was contemplated but ultimately decided against, and his wife began sending around his CV, in hope of something – anything – with greater long-term prospects.

When the Premier League rolled out their controversial and revolutionary Elite Player Performance Plan in 2012, they hired Belgian company Double Pass to handle the auditing process the new youth-football regulations required. Double Pass advertised roles for eight UK-based auditors. There were 250 applicants, of which Pepper, thanks to his wife, was one.

To his surprise, Pepper was selected for interview. To his even greater surprise, he was offered one of the eight positions. His new role saw him travelling the country, meeting with coaches, directors, managers, explaining the new governance policy, what was required of clubs and how they would be marked against a set of strict criteria. Pepper enjoyed this new responsibility immensely, meeting like-minded football people, broadening his horizons and fattening his contacts book. But there was one manager's door he remembers being slightly intimidated to knock.

'It was a bit of a moment,' Pepper, a boyhood Manchester United fan, recalls of his first meeting with Sir Alex Ferguson. 'I actually froze for about a minute. It felt like about ten.

'I thought, "I'm not going to be nervous" – until he actually walked into the room and sat down. We had a little introduction. I was supposed to tell him about the company and what we were about. I just couldn't remember it.'

Pepper soon became comfortable sitting opposite even his most prestigious clients, though, and developed a deep knowledge of EPPP's intricacies. After two years with Double Pass, he was promoted to national project manager. But over time, the repetition of the role began to grate. When a vacancy for an academy manager at Burnley was advertised, he grasped the chance for change. 'I'd done four and a half years of the auditing, and I think it has a shelf life,' he explains. 'It was almost like *Groundhog Day*, going into the same clubs, asking the same questions. I was probably ready for a change. I met with Dave Baldwin, the CEO, and got the job.'

The Burnley role represented a welcome break from the monotony of auditing, but Pepper's new gig brought a fresh and significant set of challenges. Burnley's academy – graded Category Three at the time – had been ranked the second-worst at its level in the country on its last audit, above only Morecambe. With a lack of players being developed for the first team, the academy was a money pit and an irrelevance.

'It was an academy that was running quite in silo to the main club,' Pepper says. 'They'd just started the development squad.

That was a good initiative, to get together a group of under-23s and start supporting the first team and try and increase their footprint within the Football League, because their productivity was so low. They hadn't had a player since Jay Rodriguez who'd significantly played in the first team. But all the academy staff were based over at Turf Moor. It was very disjointed.

'We went through an audit within a few months of me getting in the building. We had to try and get in line with everyone. Then we went through another audit a few months later and got Cat Two status. I've been here three years now, and we're applying for Cat One this year. The academy wasn't really on the radar the year I came. Some of the staff that were here then said they were playing on Sunday-league pitches. The youth team didn't train on grass; they trained on Astroturf. We've been on an upward trajectory, hence what you see today and where we're going. We're applying for Cat One status, and hopefully we'll get it and go into the Cat One games programme next year. Some of the staff that have been here for a while can't really believe the transformation.'

Burnley's Category One status was rubber-stamped in July 2020, making them the twenty-fifth club to attain the highest rank. The club's leap from Category Three in just three years has been powered by significant investment. The Barnfield Training Centre, which the academy and first team share, opened for use in 2017 and reportedly cost £10.5million to build. Although figures vary, the yearly cost of running a Category One programme has increased significantly since the original EPPP literature estimated an outlay of between £2.5million and £4.9million in 2012. The emergence of Dwight McNeil in Burnley's first team in 2018, then, was a timely boost for the academy, convincing the club's money men that the investment is justified.

McNeil was signed in 2014, after being released by Manchester United. The winger was by no means a talent earmarked for future

Premier League stardom at that stage, but he developed steadily with Burnley and is now an England under-21 international worth upwards of £20million.

'Dwight has been in our academy since he was fourteen, albeit he's come from United, but if we didn't have an academy we wouldn't have got him,' Pepper says. 'Now we have this asset where the board of directors are probably thinking, "Wow, if we do sell him, we're going to get X amount." Behind the scenes we were talking about going Cat One, and that sort of cemented the argument, to say, "Look, we've got Dwight in the first team, let's push and let's be the best we can be, then we're not going to lose players, and if we do lose a player, we get good compensation for them." And we can attract better players as well. We can attract a few more Dwights if they get released. We've got a number in the system at the moment. People don't see it as a step down now. It's a sideways step to Burnley.

'You speak to any academy manager, once you get a player break through – and I mean a real breakthrough, not just a sub's appearance or something like that – it's something to cling to. It helps us justify our role. It lifts everyone. His peer group, it helps motivate them, gets an extra ten or twenty per cent out of them. I've been at clubs before where the first-team manager has shown no interest in academy players, and you can just sense that they almost down tools mentally because they see no pathway there. That's certainly not happened here. Even if players don't get in the first team, there's now more players getting a career within the game. Our footprint within the [Football] League is increasing, which is what we need to do.'

Their Category One status makes Burnley a unique proposition for prospective recruits. Viewed from the outside, especially at first-team level, they are something of a relic – an old-school club unspoiled by modernity; a throwback to a bygone era. Their home stadium, Turf Moor, seats just shy of 22,000 fans, modest by

Premier League standards. Although it has undergone renovations down the years, Turf Moor sits in the exact spot where it was first constructed, almost 140 years ago, and its architecture, with four separate rectangular stands, is a world removed from the identikit bowl design of contemporary arenas. In Dyche, Burnley have eschewed the current clamour for stylish continental tacticians and stayed faithful to a manager who has delivered two Premier League promotions built on methods some would consider archaic. The gravel-voiced former centre-half is a gruff authoritarian and a devotee of 4-4-2 – the traditional formation of English football since the 1960s and a shape the club's academy coaches believe is still best for having young players learn the game.

Yet Burnley boast one of the country's most impressive and borderline-opulent training facilities. The expansion and modernisation of the club's academy has been driven in no small part by Dyche's support and a search for technical improvement and marginal gains no less committed than any of his more on-trend contemporaries.

Burnley are at once a homely, small-town club punching above their weight and an established top-tier operation embracing modernity and innovation.

'Burnley is a small town,' Pepper says. 'Everyone in Burnley supports Burnley, so Burnley has almost like a village feel. You come into the club, it's still got that feel to it. We're in the Premier League, but we're very small in terms of how we operate. You only have to go over to Turf Moor, and you see the different departments: they're not big, massive plc departments at Premier League clubs. We try and recreate that here. There's a very personal approach. You can call it a family approach. What does that mean? It probably means that everyone knows each other and you feel part of something.

'We've got everything that a big club has – the quality of the pitches, the facilities, the staff. It's that little bit of a personal touch. And also a pathway. We have cut our number down. We're not about numbers. It's about quality over quantity. We're not known for spending fortunes on young players. We don't do that; we don't spend money on young players at the moment. We signed a young player from Spurs at under-16, and said to him, "If you do well, rest assured that there's not going to be a right-back coming in at the year above that we've spent half a million on. That's not going to happen." It's trying to sell that pathway. And once players come in, they enjoy it; they enjoy the programme, they enjoy how the staff work, they play lots of football. They get lots of opportunities to develop and shine, and then there's a pathway. They get into our under-23s a little bit quicker. Last year we had two under-16s playing regularly in under-23 football. Ben Woods, who came from Man United, he was playing under-23 football last year. There's a quicker pathway here if you are a good player.'

Their Category One certification is fresh enough that, right now, Burnley's academy is still in a growth phase. In theory, the next stage will see a higher calibre of young player attracted to their programme, and, slowly but surely, the pipeline that fed McNeil into the first team will begin to gush. That's when the return on the club's investment will be reaped. Pepper is aware of those expectations, even if it's an element of his role with which he is not entirely at ease. 'I see myself as a developer,' he says. 'I always look at people or players as development projects, but that's not always the case. We are a business, and sometimes you have to make business decisions. The priority for me is to treat people right, give them a great experience. It's a harsh industry.

'There's a business head that you have to have on, and then your own personal philosophy. There's a lot of conflict there with my own outlook. I think developing people is really important, whether they're players or staff, but treating people right. Players are seen as commodities. If you're a good player, you get treated differently, you get spoken to more. I see that so much. That doesn't sit right with me.

'But then you've got that business head. We've got to produce footballers. We've got to get a return on investment. That will become more apparent in the next few years. We're in a cycle at the moment of just improving standards, as we've gone from Cat Three to Cat One. There hasn't really been a lot of targets. The target has been quite clear: improve. We've shown that, and Dwight being in the first team has taken the pressure off a little bit. But that business model, getting a return on investment, is going to be more paramount in future years here. That's something that I wrestle with.'

Managing a Category One academy means being responsible for the day-to-day running and future planning of a multi-million-pound business, and balancing that with the welfare of dozens of employees and hundreds of young people. The skills of business and personnel-management this requires have been learned on the job.

The personal principles Pepper finds at odds with the harsher realities of his role were formulated long ago. The world of youth development has evolved to the point it would be almost unrecognisable to that teenager who set his sights on a coaching career as he recovered from a broken leg nearly three decades ago. Pepper has to think hard to remember how it felt to be that young man, to feel the desire that kept him drawn to football – the game, rather than the business – when fate tried to push him away.

'I'm a frustrated coach,' he admits. 'In an ideal world, if everyone was paid the same, and you asked what role would I want, I'd pick coaching. That's my passion. That's what I enjoy. I've got a great role, but is it the most exciting role within the academy? Probably not. It's probably the most varied. No day is the same. I went to another club in the area yesterday with our head of recruitment to have a meeting about players. Then next day I'm doing interviews for our education officer. The next day I'm dealing with budgets. The next day I'm talking with the coaches about a triallist coming in. Every day is different, which I quite like. I quite like the flexibility.

'I actually get to the point where I'm fed up of the tracksuit.'

***

'That made us realise, hey, it is an unfair game,' Rasmus Ankersen, Brentford's director of football, said in 2016 as he remembered the epiphany that led to the club's decision to close their academy programme.

Ankersen was referring to Brentford's loss of a pair of star academy players to bigger, richer, more powerful clubs: skilful midfielder Ian Carlo Poveda, who left for Manchester City, and striker Joshua Bohui, who joined Manchester United. With neither player old enough to have been offered a professional contract at the time, the buying clubs were bound only to pay fees for the standout teens in accordance with the compensation structure stipulated under EPPP. Brentford claim they received just £30,000 for each player.

Of the alternative options the club considered when discussing the closure of their Category Two academy, they settled upon a B-team model. Instead of running age-group teams from under-9s to under-23s, they would remove themselves from EPPP and its games programme altogether, constructing a squad of players in their late teens – some might have been released from other academies; some might have slipped through the scouting net altogether – and have them play prestige friendlies against high-calibre domestic and European opposition.

'It allowed us far more flexibility on how we do that because we are not as restricted by regulations or rules,' Robert Rowan,

Brentford's former technical director who died suddenly in 2018, aged just twenty-eight, told *The Guardian*. 'It was the most sustainable and effective option. It's a lot easier to assess something that has got a turnaround of three years than over ten years. Once that is over we will more than likely review again and see what we need to do differently to achieve our goal.'

The change Brentford made has saved the club around £1.5million per year. Echoing Brentford's frustration with EPPP and seeing the boost the new model had given the London side's bank balance, other clubs were inspired to rethink their approach to youth development.

Huddersfield Town were one such club. In 2017, with the Yorkshire side thriving and defying expectations in the Premier League, then-chairman Dean Hoyle made the decision to downgrade the club's academy from Category Two to Category Four, disbanding the lower age groups and predominantly focusing, similarly to Brentford, on players aged seventeen and up.

'My understanding of what [Hoyle's] reason was is he didn't feel it was working at the time,' says David Webb, Huddersfield's former director of football. 'I don't think he was a big believer in it. He was still a big believer in the academy system, but not that progression. He felt that he wanted to go down a model of under-16s and above, bring those age groups closer to the first team, so the ones they did have would still have those first-team opportunities.

'He was for keeping the academy, but for the older age groups. My understanding was that he wanted to get more players into the first team and he felt this was a better way of doing it. He had looked at Brentford's model and he probably looked at a couple of other models abroad. He felt that would be the best way of getting players into the first team quicker. He thought they would be more noticeable if they're sixteen, seventeen, eighteen. And give them more of a focus, that was his thinking.

'There are a lot of pluses with that type of model. I can understand why Brentford did it. One of the main things that I spoke to Rasmus about was, because of the area they were in, in west London, they were getting swamped by Arsenal, Chelsea, Tottenham, West Ham. A lot of bigger clubs were just cherry-picking their best players at thirteen, fourteen, fifteen, even younger. He said, "We're developing these players but they're getting picked off so early, so we're just basically developing them for other clubs." The model they decided they'd go for was what they called a late-seed model. They'd keep a B team and invest in that heavily. The B team and the first team are very connected. They train the same way. Huddersfield, over the next two or three years, will try to emulate that model.'

For all the business sense it made for Brentford and Huddersfield to tear up their academy programmes, the decision came with a real human cost. More than 100 kids at each club were released, with dozens of staff members – coaches, physios, support staff – made redundant. The parents of the children let go felt the clubs had been callous, cutting short the dreams of so many without warning.

The way Brentford, Huddersfield and other clubs who've followed a similar course of action see it, though, they will no longer peddle an impossible dream en masse, on account of the fact only half of one per cent of the boys who enter an academy at under-9s level will ever make it through to the first team. According to a 2021 report by the *i* newspaper, ninety-eight per cent of those given a scholarship contract at sixteen are no longer playing within English football's top five tiers two years later. The PFA's research (83 per cent) and a 2014 BBC report (75 per cent) estimate a slightly lower attrition rate among scholarship players, but even these more conservative numbers are alarmingly high. The sheer number of players within the academy system – estimated to be around 12,000 – means the vast majority are somewhat cruelly considered mere 'bodies', whose presence is essential in aiding the development of the gifted few. By selecting and developing only players with genuine first-team potential, the mass heartbreak necessitated by the standard academy model is eradicated.

'Hopefully now academies will go down the route of, if they've got a lot of sixteen-year-olds, they should be retaining a lot more than they're releasing,' Webb says. 'If they're releasing a lot at sixteen, that will say a lot about the way they work. Obviously, someone is not doing what they're supposed to be doing who's in charge of those formative ages. Getting to sixteen, you should have more scholarships than less. You can't always get them through, but you should have a high rate. There might be the odd two or three who aren't quite there, which is natural, not the other way around, which it is at most clubs.

'The investment that Huddersfield made when I was there for a couple of younger players at sixteen, seventeen would be ones that they saw as having the potential to get in the first team. Having the development squad was very much with the idea of doing what Brentford do, having them train more or less side by side [with the first team]. The programme runs alongside.'

This new methodology has proven extremely productive for Huddersfield. In the first four months of the 2020-21 season alone, ten graduates of their revamped youth system made at least one appearance for the club's first team.

In 2020, as Burnley, Crystal Palace and Leeds United all successfully upgraded their academy offerings to attain Category One status, several clubs followed Brentford and Huddersfield's lead in drastically reducing theirs. Financially troubled Bolton Wanderers, who just three years earlier had the fourth-most-productive Category One programme in the country according to an EPPP audit, downgraded all the way to Category Four. Salford City, part-owned by five prestigious graduates of Manchester United's youth system, further reduced their Category Four system by stripping away their under-18s team. And Birmingham City, less than six months after selling seventeen-year-old homegrown star Jude Bellingham to Borussia Dortmund for £25million, announced they'd be closing their academy in favour of a model similar to Brentford's, citing the impact of the coronavirus pandemic and the UK's exit from the European Union as factors contributing to their decision.

'Maybe this Covid situation and the financial impact it's had will get clubs to look at things and strategise their way of thinking differently,' Webb says, suggesting the long financial recovery from the pandemic might quicken other clubs' decisions to step away from the conventional academy system.

'I think certain clubs will have their thinking heads on. I don't think there's going to be a set way. Some clubs will see it as a cost saving. Some clubs will see it as a better way of getting young players into their first team. I think now, with what's gone on, a lot of clubs will look to get younger players into their first team more. How they do it – whether they continue with a whole academy system from seven all the way through to under-23s, or they go from under-12s, even under-16s – they'll all have their own views on that.'

It would be naïve to claim the primary motive behind these clubs' decisions to close or reduce their academy programmes is anything other than fiscal. These are, primarily, cost-cutting measures. But they are also, on some level, an attempt to reboot a flawed system.

CHAPTER ELEVEN

LA MASIA OF THE LOWER LEAGUES

COLIN GORDON SITS upright in his chair. His shoulders are square and relaxed. His gaze is fixed in unwavering eye contact. In a gentle West Midlands accent that sends each word bouncing into the next like a tumbling row of dominoes, he speaks with the deliberateness of a man certain he commands keen attention. His words are given robust authority by his vast and varied experience. Gordon's long and winding career within football has seen him wear enough different hats to exhaust a milliner. As a powerful, six-foot-one striker, he represented Swindon Town, Reading, Birmingham City and more than a dozen others. He has been a manager, a coach to England's motorised-wheelchair team, and was the co-founder of a sports agency that once represented Steve McClaren, David James and Theo Walcott.

Now, on a bright Thursday morning as the spring of 2019 edges toward summer, he is sitting at his desk in the front offices of Kidderminster Harriers' Aggborough Stadium. Gordon concluded his playing career with the Worcestershire side in the early 1990s. He returned in 2015 as director of youth development, before buying a controlling stake in the club months later and installing himself as chairman. He periodically permits himself a faint smile as he details his grand plans.

Those plans centre around the construction of a new stadium; designs of which are displayed prominently around his office. The development of a Football League-quality academy and an on-site university campus are also crucial components of the ambitious project. While a handful of professional clubs with far greater means have come to view the operation of a youth system as an unjustifiable cost, Gordon considers the importance of Kidderminster's academy – as well as the club's educational offering and partnership with a local college – to be twofold. Firstly, it adheres to what the chairman considers his club's duty to provide opportunities to the area's young people. Secondly, he is hopeful a thriving academy, regularly producing players for the first team and for sale to clubs in the top four divisions, will help attract the kind of investment required if Kidderminster are to claw their way out of the National League North and, eventually, back into the Football League for the first time since 2005.

'We had none,' Gordon says of the state in which he found the club's youth-development programme in 2015. 'We farmed it out to some good guys, but they were parents who were managing teams. It was like a Sunday club. It wasn't a professionally run club. We had to change the profile. Obviously, when you change things, you get a bit of friction. We changed things around. We brought in coaches that we paid for to run the team. The minimum was B-Licence coaches, and everyone coached to a philosophy we believed in.'

That philosophy comprises forty-one slides in a digital presentation document. It breaks down, into remarkably specific detail, what is expected of Kidderminster's players in all phases of the game. It is stated that a 4-3-3 formation is to be utilised, for example; a flow chart specifies how the team should attack depending on the shape of the opposition; passing combinations are diagrammed using Barcelona and Spain as references, wide players are demanded to show the 'qualities of a defensive midfielder and skills of a winger', and the image of a pitch broken up into five horizontal 'corridors' explains where each player should station themselves in each phase of play.

'We started to produce talent and coach and work with a purpose,' Gordon continues, 'rather than a parent picking a team and it's just all about winning a game. We changed the profile and we changed the philosophy of it all, and it's bearing fruit.

'The priority is that everybody believes in what we're doing and they develop their talent and fulfil their potential. Firstly, can we get players through to our first team? If they get through to our first team, they'll automatically attract attention because of their age. Are they going to hold down a regular first-team place, or are they going to be attractive to the market and have choice?

'We're picking up a lot of kids who've failed at academy level or failed at under-21s or under-23s. For whatever reason, they haven't been given the care and attention, or they haven't been given the opportunity. The opportunity is blocked up by a lot of overseas imports. And when they do get the chance, they end up being worth far more than the overseas imports and costing a lot more money. That's not just our model. That's the model right the way through football at the moment. These kids are getting decisions made early on them and their hearts broken, and oftentimes too early. They just needed a bit of care and attention. Some of them just needed to grow and fill out their frames, some of them needed to become mentally stronger, and some of them needed to become more tactically aware. They grow up quicker in an environment like ours.

'It's a huge outlay and a huge commitment to people. But what we wanted to do was to find local talent and convince local talent that the better route might be to come with us, rather than join a

West Brom or a Wolves, or even a Walsall or a Shrewsbury. In a lot of cases now, we're winning. They can see the fruits of our labours. What we need now is facilities. We're investing heavily in facilities and infrastructure. Hopefully we can get the rewards for our first team, and those kids can get better care and attention than they maybe would do if they were with a bigger organisation.'

Kidderminster's academy shares training space with the first team, at the ostentatiously named Centre of Sporting Excellence. The training ground – where the planned new stadium and adjoining academy will be situated – is found a short drive across town from Aggborough, tucked inconspicuously behind an industrial estate. The facility is vast for a club of this level, with multiple full-size pitches, a large canteen area and ample office space across two floors. But it lacks floodlighting and the kind of all-weather 3G pitches boasted by the academies of Kidderminster's bigger-budget neighbours. The lack of a sprinkler system left the pitches scorched by an arid spell the previous summer.

In the echoing, empty canteen, academy manager Mark Muddyman plots the micro and the macro: drawing up the coming week's training schedule, and mapping out the next phase of the academy's growth in accordance with Gordon's ideals. The thirty-year-old, whose relative youth is belied by a dense black beard, was a young player with Birmingham City, Cheltenham and Yeovil before his prospects were shattered at seventeen by the diagnosis of an inflammatory condition in his joints. 'Ability as well,' he admits. 'I wasn't going to be good enough.' Quickly committing to youth coaching, he went on to work in the academies of Birmingham and Watford. He coached Jude Bellingham and Jadon Sancho, both of whom went on to find stardom with Borussia Dortmund in Germany's Bundesliga and are now England internationals. In December 2017, he became Kidderminster's academy manager, his first such role.

'When I came in for the interview, I was blown away by the ambition,' Muddyman says of his first impression of Gordon's Kidderminster project. 'It felt like a Football League club already. That felt like something I wanted to be a part of.

'We produce players in line with what the club believe. I personally believe the environment, the pitch that you're playing on, the standard of player you've got, all have to be taken into consideration before you can develop what your playing philosophy is. You can't go and play like Man City if you've not got the best players in the league or your pitch is not very good. In youth development, I think your philosophy has got to be what it is at the club. I bought into that, and that's why I came here.'

In addition to his previous roles with Birmingham and Watford, Muddyman combines his demanding Kidderminster remit with a part-time scouting gig with Manchester United's academy. He has seen first-hand how elite youth set-ups operate, and he is committed to ensuring, so far as the limits of their facilities allow, that Kidderminster aspire to the same standards. 'There's a lot of teams and stuff going on,' he says of his busy schedule. 'I've got to run the recreational side of the programme, the development side of the programme and the elite side of the programme. Pretty much nine to five, every day, unless there's a night game or a first-team game to go to. In the morning, I'll come in, find out who's ill, who's not here. I make sure everything is set for the coaches to deliver the best possible sessions at lunchtime. There's a lot of admin and coordinating matches, recruiting players and dealing with disciplinary issues, league admin or whatever it may be – planning ahead, scouting and different things. We coach at lunchtime, have a debrief with the staff and put plans in place for the following day.

'In terms of what I'm measured on or what is my aim, it's to get as many players into the first team and contributing, and for them then to generate sell-on value if possible. At this level, that's a big, big thing. I've been here eighteen months. The first six months was planning for the first full year, recruitment and getting players in the door. Now we've had one full season at it, we've changed a lot of things and brought in a lot of ideas. It's heading in the right direction.'

Kidderminster's tight budget and threadbare senior squad mean the pathway between the academy and the first team is a wide-open and well-trodden road. Whether making up the numbers in training, filling out the substitutes' bench on matchdays or being named in the starting line-up, opportunity will knock often and insistently for the club's young players.

Such a ready route to the first team is one of Kidderminster's unique selling points when it comes to persuading players to pick them over bigger local clubs. But it also means the youngsters they sign might need to be steeled for the senior game sooner than would be the case elsewhere. It's Muddyman's job to ensure that sixth-tier football does not elicit a rude awakening for the players he puts forward for first-team consideration; especially those who have come from higher-level academies and thus perhaps envisioned their introduction to the senior game in cushier surrounds. 'One thing I know from working with players at this age – especially at this level – physically, they have to go through a huge transformation before they can cope with men's football,' he says. 'Getting them up to the intensity and the fitness levels is first and foremost when they first come through the door. Once they're fit, getting them into a strength-and-conditioning programme and turning them into a man, not as soon as possible but as soon as is right for their growth and maturation rates.

'A lot of them come in the door very good, because they've been in the academy system already, or they've been coached well elsewhere. If they haven't, it's correcting those bad habits. Often, they come in technically very good. It's often the tactical understanding [they lack]. I find players who come to me if they've come out of the academy system are very good in possession, but out of possession, sometimes they need to improve. They need to develop that workrate and that understanding of what it's like going into an environment where people's livelihoods and whose mortgages are paid by football. That's very different to a seventeen-year-old who's just come out of school and is playing because he wants to be a footballer. They don't really get it.

'Psychologically and physically preparing them for men's football, it's tough, because they're not men yet and you can't talk to them like men. I would never dig someone out in front of the whole group or try and humiliate them, but I do think it is important to make them realise: if you do that in a first-team environment, it will not be accepted. You've got to make that pretty clear, set the standards higher than what they previously may have been. We want to say, "Look, we want to recreate a first-team environment, without excluding the fact that you're not quite there yet." There's a lot of stories in football about under-18s players being spoken to like they're twenty-five. You've got to be careful.'

A teenage midfielder named Jaiden White is pointed to as the emblem of how the Kidderminster academy operates and what it hopes to achieve. White was on the books of Wolverhampton Wanderers' academy until he was fifteen and spent a year with Coventry City before signing for Kidderminster ahead of the 2018-19 season. He was given a first-team debut midway through that campaign, aged just sixteen. After signing a first professional contract in the days after his seventeenth birthday, he has become a semi-regular face in the first team and has spent time on loan with Stafford Rangers to boost his readiness for senior non-league football.

'He's probably already trained with the first team, I would say, a hundred times since he left school, and he's only just turned seventeen,' Muddyman enthuses. 'That's quite unique. You don't get that with a lot of clubs at this level.'

'He loves it here,' adds Gordon. 'He's been to big clubs. They all rejected him. Now it looks like he's going to be a top, top player. The agents have started to pick the phone up and started to speak to the family and all the rest of it. They haven't scouted him. They'll have read that he's only seventeen and a few days – "Wow, he must be . . ." That's the way people are. We'll have phone calls from clubs now about him, and they won't have seen him play.

'We don't have agents here,' continues Gordon. His disdain for aspects of his former trade is clear. He is openly scornful of the kind of disreputable agents he has encountered, who offer inducements to parents, promising mortgages will be paid off or new cars purchased in exchange for a boy's signature. 'We're dealing with kids. We're here with a big net, catching them at any age. Hopefully the boys we have at our level aren't really on the radar of many clubs. And if they are, it isn't the Man Citys or Man Uniteds.'

The net Kidderminster are casting will aim to ensnare the best local female talent, too. The girls' academy will consist of two teams: an under-19s and an under-23s. The club has an established amateur ladies' side that has enjoyed success locally in recent years, but the purpose of the girls' academy is rooted in its educational offering, rather than as a supply line of talent to the women's team. The under-19s combine a full-time training programme with study towards a BTEC sports qualification, and the under-23s work towards a degree in football business management and coaching.

The girls' teams will be based at the Centre of Sporting Excellence, alongside the men's senior team and academy. It will be known as the Jill Scott KHFC Academy, bearing the name of the England international defender who has been signed up to endorse and, occasionally, coach within the programme. Tasked with recruiting the players the girls' academy will comprise and designing it's day-to-day training regimen, though, is Siobhan Hodgetts.

'The boys' programme, they've got 120 boys in six teams. The girls' programme won't be that big because the boys have got that end goal of trying to get in the Kiddy first team or trying to get out into different clubs,' Hodgetts explains, speaking in the months leading up to the girls' academy's planned launch at the beginning of the 2019-20 season. 'The female game is not as big as that yet, so what we're trying to base this on is the education.

'What you'll find the females like to do or go into – full-time university, to go to the States. You might get the odd one or two who go and play in the Super League as well. For me, it's one of the best programmes I've seen because the girls will train three, four times a week, they'll play games on a Wednesday, they'll get their own strength-and-conditioning programme. We're looking to get Jill Scott involved. She'll be a bit of a mentor, working with the girls and giving them advice. She'll come and do a couple of sessions with the girls. She came and did a session at the start, in October, then we took a group of girls to Manchester to watch City versus Blues. That's the start.'

Prior to joining Kidderminster, Hodgetts had worked for The Albion Foundation, West Brom's outreach programme, since leaving school in the mid-2000s. The only break in her association with the West Midlands club – which continues alongside her role with Kidderminster in the form of coaching at the club's own female academy – came via an eighteen-month stay in the United States, where she ran a junior team. That experience not only prepared her for the rigours of the recruitment drive she now oversees but also affirmed the importance of fostering a comfortable social environment for a group of youngsters unfamiliar to one another. 'On Saturday I'm taking a group of girls to watch England Ladies play, so it's not just football, it's the social side,' she says. 'So, when they do come in in September, it's not so daunting a new environment and they might know somebody already. Loads of open evenings. Loads of presentations. Parents can come in as well. If they've got any questions about the football, the education side, there's always staff here to help out.

'They do two years of playing full-time football. There's a lot of these programmes about. For the girls here, they'll train three or four times a week, so there's more football involved. For the girls who want to push their football and keep developing and really want to try and get into a semi-pro or pro, this is a good programme for it.'

Kidderminster has been synonymous with the carpet industry since the 1800s. A post-war boom in the 1950s, 60s and 70s saw the town's carpet factories employ as many as 15,000 people. The industry has declined significantly in recent decades, though. Many of the factories have been shut down, demolished and replaced by car parks and supermarkets. It is now estimated that Kidderminster's five remaining carpet factories combined employ as few as 500 people. The demise of the carpet industry meant a crippling loss of work for the town but also an erosion of its identity. Gordon is hopeful the football club can fill the void.

An invitation to lecture at the University Campus of Football Business (UCFB) base at Wembley Stadium was a light-bulb moment for Gordon. The UCFB began in the relatively humble setting of Burnley's Turf Moor but now runs out of Wembley and Manchester City's Etihad Stadium, giving students the opportunity to study for sports-specific degrees with proximity and access to high-class sporting environments and industry expertise. Why not replicate the model at Kidderminster's planned new stadium, he thought, only going one step further?

'Fantastic kids, brilliant kids,' Gordon remembers of his Wembley visit, 'but no practical experience. My thoughts then: if I could find a club that was full-time, that could sit at the top of this educational pyramid and give those kids these kind of experiences, then it would be very creditable to the market. No other football club does it. That was the idea and that is what we're looking to do.'

A student with designs on a career in sports management, then, could accumulate real-life experience in such roles by shadowing and working alongside Kidderminster's decision-makers; a budding physiotherapist could, literally, gain hands-on experience by helping the club's physio; those intent on becoming video analysts could help cut film and present tactical breakdowns to the academy players.

'Then they have the opportunity to work in the business of football, even if they are not going to become footballers,' Gordon continues. 'Football is a brilliant industry to be in. There are a lot of jobs, not just playing. Our aim is to help them become coaches, analysts, strength and conditioning, you name it. All aspects of football. We have a degree [programme] higher up, and at the moment we're doing BTECs for further education. We're just trying to put together an A-Level course because we're losing good, bright kids because we can't offer an A-Level course. That's the next step for us.

'The finance then generates a budget that becomes competitive. The football club becomes sustainable, where we're not relying on benefactors to put money in to keep footballers afloat. The budget can become financed by education, and the first team is feeding back into the education by providing opportunity and training. It's a cycle.

'The reason I was involved is what difference we can make to our community. Ultimately, we want to be a university. That will change the nature of the town. The town has been a carpet town for years, which it is no longer. We'll change the profile of the town. If you're bringing in a thousand university students, obviously you're bringing in a lot more revenue that wasn't here before. We want to support the town that way.

'A club like ours shouldn't have the number of staff that you're looking at today. But we are building something that, hopefully, will be successful – financially, yes, but also we should create some kind of legacy; it's our duty to. They come out and support us every other week. It's our duty to put something back into the community.'

Just five months later, though, Gordon would sell his stake in the club and step down from his position as chairman to resume a career in sports agency. He says he lost around £1.5million of his own money on the Kidderminster project and, in the end, felt he couldn't personally finance everything he wanted to achieve.

'Unfortunately, things didn't move as quickly as I would have wanted,' he says.

But the dream of a new stadium, improved academy facilities and on-site university has not died with Gordon's departure. Local businessman Richard Lane, an investor the former chairman had identified and brought on board, is, according to Gordon, 'carrying on with the plans.

'Full steam ahead.'

***

Thirty-five miles north of Kidderminster's Aggborough Stadium, across the Worcestershire–Shropshire border, David Longwell sits in an executive box overlooking the pitch at Shrewsbury Town's New Meadow home. He is explaining how Pep Guardiola, Xavi and Lionel Messi have influenced his work as the League One side's academy manager.

'I was very much influenced by Barcelona at that time. That was the big thing,' the tall, red-haired Scot says, thinking back to his time in charge of St Mirren's junior ranks. As an aspiring goalkeeper in his youth, Longwell quickly realised he had no future as a footballer and enrolled on a coaching course at a local college. His studies took him into St Mirren's academy to gain practical experience. Fifteen years later, he was still there, rising to the role of academy manager and making the humble Paisley club competitive with Old Firm powerhouses Celtic and Rangers at youth level.

'A lot of clubs would say, "We're playing like Barcelona," but they'd do it until it got difficult and then just launch it,' he continues. 'We just religiously did it. A lot of the content of the training was technical-based, decision-making-based. In the games, we made them play football. Because we made them play football, they can handle the level they're playing at. It's about being committed to your plan, being strong in your opinions of how you want to play.

'Other clubs are obsessed about winning. I wanted to win, and, looking back now, I was very demanding, sometimes over-demanding. But it was getting them to play in a certain way.'

While at St Mirren, Longwell would photocopy extracts of Johan Cruyff's autobiography and pass them around to his coaches. Studying the methods the legendary Dutchman introduced to Barcelona's famous *La Masia* youth system, Longwell demanded his staff all sing from the same hymn sheet. A scaled-down version of the Barça model was adopted. Seeing the success the Catalan club were achieving under Guardiola in the early 2010s – headlined by homegrown players such as Messi, Xavi, Andrés Iniesta and Sergio Busquets – only further cemented Longwell's commitment to the same principles of technique, playing out from the back and dominating possession.

'It was just so inspirational,' he says. 'People can say that, and it sounds a bit cheesy. But it was so inspirational to watch them. At the time in Scotland, a lot of the stuff was percentages football. It was the inspiration of, number one, the style of play, but also the inspiration of how many players they brought through. It was twofold. That was why it resonated so much with me. It was a light-bulb in my life. I wanted to become better, and, bang, Barcelona are right on the scene.

'It's something that I've changed at Shrewsbury now. Say a ball goes over the top, the defender and the striker are running for the ball and the defender kicks it out of the pitch. It kills me. It really bothers me. There's got to be something else you can do. It's a low level of how to play the game. For me, when that happens, you don't kick it out; you try and find a solution. It's easy to kick it out. And I'm not saying there aren't times in games when they're older where they'll need to. But we're going through a youth-development process.

'I used to say to people, when it was St Mirren against Rangers under-15s four years ago, "Who's going to remember the score? Who cares?" We actually got to the point at St Mirren where we were beating Rangers and Celtic on a semi-regular basis, whereas before we were getting battered, losing all the time. But the difference was that we were committed to a process. If we were just sacrificing all our stuff at the start of that and going longer, they never would have made it through that development process. We had to have that understanding with the coaches that we need to get the kids playing under pressure in training.

'If I'm demanding they play it out from the back, I can't really criticise too much. It's my responsibility. You try to take a little bit of that responsibility away to try and let them do it. They've got to be allowed to make decisions. The way I've coached for the last fifteen years is: they are part of the process; you've got to empower them to make decisions and be autonomous thinkers.'

It proved successful, not only in making St Mirren competitive on the Scottish youth-football scene, but in producing high-quality players. The standout name to have emerged from the club's academy in that period is John McGinn, the Aston Villa and Scotland playmaker, but the likes of Kenny McLean (Norwich City), Stevie Mallan, Stephen McGinn, Kyle Magennis (all Hibernian), Sean Kelly (Ross County) and Kyle McAllister (Derby County) are among those to have enjoyed successful careers either side of the border.

More recently, Longwell's development philosophy has been imbued with a strong influence almost anathema to the Barcelona way. In 2017, after a short stint as MLS side Orlando City's academy manager, he was headhunted by New York Red Bulls to run their youth set-up. Part of the drinks manufacturer's global footballing portfolio, the New York club conform to the same methods of play and recruitment as the other sides within Red Bull's empire – that is: an intense, counter-pressing brand of football, and a thirst to snap up the best, most cost-effective young talent from around the globe. Red Bull's football arm guards its secrets closely, even being known to have departing coaches sign non-disclosure agreements to prevent them discussing the intricacies of the operation's inner workings.

Longwell worked closely with Jesse Marsch, the impressive American coach who was in charge of New York Red Bulls at the time but has since moved over to the brand's Salzburg club. Longwell also spent time in Salzburg, observing how the Austrian side operate. 'It's the opposite of Barcelona and Man City,' he explains. 'But it's then how you can adapt that a little bit. The Red Bull philosophy is very much against the ball, pressing, and how you can go forward quicker. A little bit like Liverpool. How Liverpool play is how we want to play. Liverpool still build from the back, but it's not so much possession-based. That pace and that direction, it's not just going long for the sake of it. I think

Red Bull helped influence that. I take bits from there, I take bits from Orlando, I take bits from being at St Mirren. You watch Barcelona, you watch Liverpool. You take bits of everything. It's not that I'm changing everything, but you're evolving everything.'

Longwell's Stateside stay was only ever planned to be a short-term excursion. In February 2019, after being contacted by club chairman Brian Caldwell, he accepted an offer to take over Shrewsbury's Category Three academy. With a burgeoning reputation as a developer of young footballers, and with no wife or children to take into consideration, Longwell could have picked any destination on the globe for his next career move. Swapping the bustle and energy of New York for the rolling River Severn and the sleepy Shropshire market town, then, hardly seems the obvious choice. But in football terms, he insists, the move was rooted in logic.

'I thought there was a really good project here,' Longwell enthuses in his rapid-fire Renfrew accent. 'And people would say it was a bit of a surprise move, but to me it's been the best move and the right move, because there's a lot of work to be done here and I think we can implement it. I think we can make a big difference here. There's some good work that's been done and there are good foundations, but, for me, there's a lot more that can be done.

'I was pleasantly surprised with the good people here. Eric Ramsey [who has since joined Chelsea] is a really sharp, really intelligent guy. You then go to the staff in the academy. I could see these are good people. I was really enthused by the people. I then looked at what was going on. They do try and play football a certain way. You can see there's a willingness to do the right things, and there's a willingness to try and take it forward.

'People talk about philosophy. Philosophy isn't the formation. Philosophy is how you play. The philosophy for us, very simply, is: we're always going to press high, we're always going to try and go to the goal if we can, and we're always going to try and play out from the back. Those are the basics of it.'

Longwell's plan to produce a steady stream of young talent for Shrewsbury's first team is three-pronged: improve local grassroots recruitment; provide a home for the best players released by nearby Category One academies; and continue to implement his Barcelona-inspired philosophy.

'Those three things together,' he says, 'will get success.'

***

In May 2016, the parents of Brentford's academy players were gathered together and informed that the club's youth system was to undergo a restructure. They were told the academy was to close, that their sons were to be released, left to find somewhere else to grasp at the greased rope of their football dreams. It wasn't just the kids who were cut loose. Dozens of the club's academy staff, in accordance with HR protocols, had already been told that they should seek alternative employment, made redundant as part of the shake-up.

Jon De Souza was among the number displaced. He had been with Brentford since 2011. An enthusiastic young coach with a master's degree in Sport and Business Management, he'd risen through the ranks at Luton Town to become academy manager in his mid-twenties, before serving as a coaching developer and under-18s and under-21s manager at Brentford.

'We felt we were going to get ten years to get anywhere near good,' De Souza remembers of his shock at Brentford's decision to close their academy in favour of a B-team model. 'Most academies take ten years to get the staff in that's consistent and continuous. We were five years into it. I felt we had just started to get players through.

'But then the Danish director of football came in and the Danish coaches. They weren't great believers in the English academy system. I knew from the last season it was the beginning of the end. It's football. You know you're going to lose your job. The frustration for us was there were three playing in the England under-16s squad that had come from Brentford's academy. We got two centre-halves playing in the Premier League for over £40 million. We never felt we were able to get a consistent level of money or players. From a personal point of view, that was a disappointment, because I wanted to be able to see the players' full journey, from managing them at under-9, all the way through to the first team.'

De Souza's next step landed him at a club with opposite values to Brentford's when it comes to their trust in the academy system. As of the 2020-21 season, Colchester United are the only club in League Two whose academy is graded as high as Category Two under EPPP. Chairman Robbie Cowling has overseen a significant investment of cash and faith in the Essex side's youth ranks. Colchester's academy shares a home with the first team, training and playing out of the club's Florence Park training ground, with its main building in the style of a large, modern farmhouse with views over an expanse of immaculate grass pitches. In an echoing upstairs office overlooking the main training field, De Souza recounts how he came to understand Colchester's firm dedication to youth development upon becoming academy manager just two months after leaving Brentford.

'I must have done the chairman and the director of football's head in with all the questions I asked,' he says. 'I asked about everything. But I was sold the dream. It wasn't until November time, when we were second from bottom of League Two – which is real pressure, because if we drop out of the League, the academy is gone – the chairman said to us, "If we're second from bottom, we need to be playing younger players. We can't be second from

bottom playing senior players that are making mistakes anyway."
I thought that showed he was a really brave chairman to stick to
his beliefs. I don't think there's any greater pressure than being in
the bottom two of League Two.

'Since then, I've had nothing but reassurances that he's in it for
the long term and he really cares. I'm aware football can change,
and I'm sure at some point he'll look to expand the academy
or reshape it in any way, shape or form. But he's definitely, at
the moment, got youth and the local community close to his
heart. Our chairman is very passionate about young local people
playing for their local club. He's a great believer in that, on top
of the financial rewards of running a top academy. It's something
that I'm delighted to be a part of.'

With such faith and investment comes expectation. It costs
around £2.5million per year to run a Category Two academy, and
the sums pumped into Colchester's youth set-up are balanced by
the savings incurred at senior level: homegrown youngsters cost
nothing in terms of transfer fees and command a lighter wage
packet than experienced pros, even at League Two level. Cowling's
stated aim for the academy is that its graduates account for fifty
per cent of the first-team squad. 'We're measured directly on it,
in terms of squad make-up, in terms of the eighteen picked on a
Saturday, and in terms of minutes played,' De Souza says. 'We're
at fifty per cent of the squad, and we're at about forty-seven per
cent of the playing time.'

Despite their comparatively low standing on the Football
League ladder, the methods employed by Colchester in rearing
their young talent echo those found at some of the biggest clubs
in the land. As explored previously, a philosophy focused heavily
around the needs of each individual player has brought success
to Liverpool and Manchester United in the development of
Trent Alexander-Arnold and Marcus Rashford, and many of
the current gilded generation of young England internationals

will have experienced similar methodologies at their clubs. Colchester adhere strictly to such principles, perhaps even more so than many of the big-budget superstar factories.

'We're probably quite unique in that a lot of clubs say it, and we actually do it: the individual drives us,' De Souza says. 'A lot of clubs say it's about the individual, yet they've got clear styles of play, clear formations, clear everything. And there's nothing wrong with that. You might say your club is driven by the playing style, and there are some very successful clubs that are. We're driven by the individual. For me, a style of play doesn't make a debut or a player that will be sold for a lot of money; the player does. That's why the player has to be the focus of what we do.

'It's something that was here [before I arrived], but I don't think it was as strong. When I left Brentford, that eight weeks [before starting with Colchester] was probably the best eight weeks I ever had. The Colchester guys were very much, "Come here, join for three months, look at it, add to it, don't rip it apart." I didn't have a lot of work to do before I joined Colchester. It was all going to be on the job. For eight weeks I had a real reflection. I kept asking myself, "What am I as a coach?" And I kept saying, "I'm an individual coach." I looked back. I've always played 4-3-3. I've always played out from the back. Always tried to play football. I can't be about the individual if every year for the past five or six years I've done the same thing. That was a real light-bulb moment. When I came here and looked at the programme, it was about the individual, but I thought, "If we're going to do it, let's properly be driven by the individual."

'I had an argument with the academy manager at Brentford. He wanted the goalkeeper to kick it. He said he didn't want to play out – "Learn to kick it. Go longer." I was like, "No, no, no. He needs to play." On reflection, it was my ego – I wanted us to play football. The only thing that bothered me was my ego. I didn't want people to think I boot it, when, actually, the right thing for that player's development is to go longer. By the same token, if you've got a centre-forward who is struggling to deal with aerial balls, he needs to deal with that in games. If you keep going pass, pass, pass, he's not getting that. It's just a way of breaking down what a player needs. We've got to go, "Right, forget what we're trying to achieve as a club – this player needs X, Y and Z."

'The big thing I say is, "Don't coach the session. Coach the players." When you're planning, look at what the players need. If you've got a full-back who's very good at his one-v-one defending but not so good at his crossing, we've got to make him exceptional at his strength and also work on his weakness. He's not going to get that by doing a generic possession practice. He's got to work on what he needs to. We make sure we really push that. But we're aware we can't just be developing the individual. Part of that has got to be: what's the individual's role in the team?'

That's the point at which the good of the team and the good of the individual being developed must be in conversation with each other. While Colchester will adapt their style of play, bending to the developmental needs of the players, they also, where possible, recruit and mould their youngsters in accordance with their core guiding principles. Results, to an extent, can take a backseat, but a balance must be struck in instilling team principles and an appreciation of how, by the time they reach first-team readiness, the players need to know the value of three points.

'Our four pillars are: work ethic, technique, understanding, winning,' De Souza says. 'And I think it comes in that order. If they don't work hard, then they've got no chance. If they can't pass or see the ball, then it doesn't matter how much you talk about winning; they can't do it if they don't understand the game. You've got to work on their work ethic and their attitude, then their technical ability, then their technical understanding, then you've got to talk about winning, because winning is part of it. Sometimes, people focus a lot on winning, but it's irrelevant by the time they get into the first team if they don't have the technical quality. Technique is fundamental.

'Our under-18s won one game all season – and this is not me bragging – and that was three weeks ago. It went too far the other way. They've got to learn to win. But we're trying to create a way of judging the process, rather than the outcome. For us, it's about judging the process. It's too easy to say, "If you win on Saturday, you've done well." But winning is a massive thing. We say winning isn't everything, but wanting to is. The players have to want to win. Because we are so individual-based, we have a lot of conversations saying, "Are we downplaying the importance of winning?" But it has to come as the icing on the cake once you've got the other bits done.

'I think too much judging is done in football. If you believed in that player six months ago, just make him better. If you focus on making a player better, rather than judging them, you're more likely to make less mistakes.'

Colchester are hopeful that their rare combination of a high-level programme and a clear pathway to first-team football will continue to make them an attractive proposition for the area's best young talent. The likes of Southend and Cambridge, for example, might be able to rival their promise of a pathway, but they can't match Colchester's facilities and Category Two status. And the route to the senior side at Category One clubs, by comparison, tends to be clogged. Colchester also dip their toes into the London talent pool. One of their two satellite development centres is stationed in Shenfield, roughly equidistant between their main base and the capital. Thirty-three per cent of the players in their academy have come from their development centres, and they ship in players from London daily via minibus.

As attractive as their offering of first-team opportunities might be, Colchester are aware that the most gifted young players will, at best, view them as a stepping stone to greater heights. The club are comfortable with that; encouraging of it, in fact, as their ultimate goal for their homegrown youngsters, as is the case at almost every other academy in the country, is an eventual lucrative sale.

'I think the chairman wants to recoup as much money as he can,' De Souza admits. 'Our aim here, more so than most clubs, is the path to get them in the first team. The pathway is here. I'm not going to say it's easier to get in the first team here, but the pathway is clearer. If you are good enough, you will get the opportunity at this club, which can't be said of every club. Our job is to make sure that [players promoted from the academy] can help the team win and be sold. Get them in the first team. When they're in the first team, are they helping the team win and can they be sold?'

De Souza is speaking in May 2019. He is slight but athletic and just thirty-three years old. His own footballing ambitions were curtailed when he was released by Luton at eighteen. He continued to play at non-league level but found an alternate passion for coaching. Sitting in a tracksuit top and shorts, he laments that he is no longer out on the grass as much as he'd like – he leads, on average, one session a fortnight – due to the administrative demands of his role. Were his original ambitions realised, he'd likely still be playing professionally, as he's younger than some members of Colchester's first team. Instead, in just two weeks' time, he will be promoted, becoming the club's director of performance.

'The thing the chairman has brought in here is he's not just trying to promote players into the first team,' he says, perhaps, in retrospect, with some knowledge of his pending promotion, 'he's trying to promote managers. Four out of the last five managers have come from the academy. The director of football was academy manager, then became manager, now director of football. The current first-team coach was under-14s coach when he joined. The assistant first-team coach was under-13s coach when he joined. So they've come through the academy and got that affiliation with the academy.'

After dealing with the blow of being let go by Brentford, feeling as though the rug was pulled out from under him after years of work and progress, having seen the disappointment etched on the faces of the cast-off kids and their parents, is De Souza worried others will follow his former club's lead?

'One hundred per cent,' is his instant response. 'I think the amount of investment and the time it takes is always a worry. Academies are now massive, massive business organisations. It's an extensive operation and it can take time.

'In an industry now where there are a lot of foreign owners at a higher level, they need immediate success. I don't think academies are going to provide immediate success.'

CHAPTER TWELVE

BREAKING THROUGH

'NO, NO, NO. I'm not going to change anything,' Louis van Gaal told his assistants. 'Marcus is going to come in.'

It was 25 February 2016. Manchester United were preparing to face FC Midtjylland in the first knockout round of the Europa League. Having been embarrassed by a 2-1 first-leg defeat in Denmark the prior week, Van Gaal, the experienced Dutch manager in charge of United at the time, must have been aware a shock exit at this stage of Europe's secondary competition could cost him his job.

An injury to first-choice striker Anthony Martial, which the French forward sustained in the pre-match warm-up, was far from ideal preparation, then. Van Gaal gathered his lieutenants in the home dressing room in the minutes before a teamsheet for the game would have to be submitted. They discussed potential tactical shifts to account for Martial's absence, or how they could perhaps deploy an experienced back-up out of position at the point of attack.

The only natural striker United had in reserve for the game was eighteen-year-old Marcus Rashford. The teenager had impressed on his rise through the academy ranks and had spent the last two years learning the inner workings of the centre-forward position, having previously played predominantly as a winger. Still, Rashford was raw, untested. He was only named among the substitutes because Will Keane, another young, academy-bred striker who was higher in the pecking order at the time, had suffered a season-ending groin injury in an FA Cup win over Shrewsbury Town three days earlier.

Reflecting on Van Gaal's two-year reign at Old Trafford, there are plenty of aspects of the Dutchman's management to criticise. The players were over-coached to the point the football they produced was staid and stale, barely watchable. For the money the club spent in the two summer transfer windows he oversaw, a highest league finish of fourth and an FA Cup triumph represented a meagre return on investment. But Van Gaal's faith in United's young players was unimpeachable. In two years, he handed competitive debuts to fifteen academy graduates, including Jesse Lingard, Andreas Pereira and, against Midtjylland, Rashford.

'He's capable of doing it. I'm confident in that,' Van Gaal told his coaches after deciding that Rashford would not only get his first taste of senior football versus the Danes but he would do so as a member of the starting line-up.

'I had to explain to [Rashford] the set pieces,' remembers Frans Hoek, one of Van Gaal's assistants at United. 'I went to him. I looked him in the eyes. Of course, he must have been nervous, but it didn't show. He was concentrated on what he had to do. He looked good. He looked confident. He was looking forward to it. He made a very strong impression on me. That look in his eyes, it was, "OK, I have a chance now and I can show them." It went very well with him.'

Very well indeed. He scored twice in a 5-1 win. So impressed was Van Gaal by the teenager's performance that he selected Rashford to start against Arsenal in the Premier League three days later; Rashford again scored twice.

Rashford's lightning-bolt arrival into senior football saw him chosen as part of England's squad for Euro 2016 at the end of the season. He has been a key figure for club and country ever since. It is interesting to ponder how things might have played out for him had Keane and Martial not fallen injured, though. Such a talent would surely have earned a first-team shot at some stage, but the conditions might not have been so favourable. A debut against higher-calibre opponents, in which he would likely have been afforded only a few minutes as a late substitute – a more typical introduction for a teenage debutant – would have proven more difficult to make an impact. And the following season, Van Gaal was replaced as United manager by José Mourinho, who, it is fair to say, does not have a reputation equal to the Dutchman's when it comes to blooding young players. Rashford had long been considered one of the brightest prospects within United's academy, and his development had been carefully managed and nurtured to give him the best possible chance of making the grade at first-team level, yet still his successful transition to the senior game relied on a set of serendipitous circumstances.

The emergence at Crystal Palace of Aaron Wan-Bissaka, now a team-mate of Rashford's with United, is a similar story. The England full-back was a late convert to his ultimate position, having previously been a winger. At twenty, he was being lined up for a loan move to a Championship club to gain first-team experience, either in readiness for an eventual Palace debut or a move elsewhere. Those plans were nixed, however, when Palace suffered a spate of injuries in February 2018. Wan-Bissaka was drafted into Roy Hodgson's senior squad for an unenviable run of fixtures – taking on Manchester United, Arsenal and Tottenham within the space of thirteen days – and thrived. He locked down a first-team berth and earned the club's Player of the Year honour at the end of his first full senior campaign.

Academy manager Gary Issott, who oversaw Wan-Bissaka's rise from a winger considered for release at fourteen to a £50million first-team star, has been with Palace through times of prosperity and struggle. In his decade and a half at the club, he has learned the primary objective of his role as academy director, to produce players for the first team, is easier when the club are down on their luck. 'We were lucky because when we got relegated and didn't go back up the year after, and Iain [Dowie, Palace's manager at the time] left, the parachute money and the quality of the squad lessened – Andy Johnson was sold, Fitz Hall was sold,' Issott remembers of Palace's drop into the Championship in 2005. 'That's when the opportunities for the young players came. In that youth team, we had Victor Moses, John Bostock, Sean Scannell, Nathaniel Clyne. All these boys got opportunities in the Championship that they probably wouldn't have got had we stayed in the Premier League.

'That helped me, because it meant I got players in the team and I built that reputation that I was able to get young players in the club. The best period we had was under Neil Warnock. The team was experiencing financial difficulties under [owner] Simon Jordan, and eventually he was to lose the club, but that's when they couldn't buy any players in the transfer window and they had no alternative but to turn to the young players at the club.

'The real fulfilment of doing your role is when a young player goes in [the first team] and stays in. It's odd because you see these boys at thirteen or fourteen and you know how different they look to the public. Also, you know where they've come from, what they've been through. Wan-Bissaka to the public now is a superstar, but I can remember him as a shy kid who was struggling at school. Or [if] a young player leaves you and goes and has a great career – a bit like [George] Boyd all them years ago at Stevenage [where Issott previously coached]. On a Saturday, I'll be travelling back from a game and I'll look at teamsheets on my phone to see if Boydie's played today. And you'll look for all the lads, in all the games.'

Without exception, the coaches and academy managers interviewed for this book agree that the greatest thrill their role provides is the moment one of their young players breaks through to the first team. But the pathway between the academy and the senior side is narrow at Premier League clubs, many of whom also happen to run the highest-calibre youth programmes in the country. The difference between each league position is worth millions of pounds in prize money; relegation can be a slippery slope to insolvency and European qualification brings a boost of tens of millions in income. The stakes are high, and managers, understandably, are risk-averse. Young players take time to mature, to learn the game through a process of trial and error. Safer, more experienced alternatives are sought via the transfer market.

There has been an increase in the opportunities given to young, academy-bred players in the Premier League recently. In the 2019-20 season, sixty-two homegrown players – defined as those who have spent at least three years with an English club before the age of twenty-one – made Premier League debuts. That represented a fifty-one per cent increase on the previous campaign. There was also a thirty-five per cent increase in the game time these players, on average, received, as well as a fifty-two per cent uptick in the average minutes played by all homegrown players aged twenty-three and under. The Premier League's end-of-season report attributed this growth in opportunity for young players to the success of EPPP and the £800million post-2012 investment in youth football's facilities and staffing made by clubs and governing bodies.

Yet still many of the best young talents are looking abroad, to the Bundesliga in particular, for sustained first-team opportunities at the highest level. There appears a greater trust of young players in Germany, where, according to Transfermarkt.com, the average player age of top-flight squads is just 25.6 years. In the Premier League, the average is 27.1 years. What's more, as of February 2021, nine Bundesliga squads – including three of the division's Champions League regulars: Borussia Dortmund (25.3), Bayer Leverkusen (25.4) and RB Leipzig (24.4) – have an average age under 25.6 years. Zero Premier League clubs have such a low age composition. It's no wonder the likes of Jadon Sancho and Jude Bellingham (Dortmund), Jamal Musiala (Bayern Munich), Reece Oxford (Augsburg) and Rabbi Matondo (Schalke) flocked to Germany for their big break.

In light of the difficulty even England's best youngsters have found in cracking the country's top-tier senior sides, youth coaches and academy managers have come to redefine what they consider success. 'It's how many players you develop for the game, that's what you should be judged on,' Issott argues. 'At some clubs, it's so difficult to get players in [to the first team], but they've got players all through the Football League. There should be credit given for that.'

'A career is a career,' adds Gareth Taylor, who in his time as Manchester City's under-18s manager saw several top prospects give up hope of a future at the Etihad and seek opportunities elsewhere. 'Ideally, they make it into our first team, but if not, we should be just as proud of Brahim Diaz going to Real Madrid, or Rabbi going to Schalke, or Jadon. At the end of the day, it's difficult. We're talking about one of the top teams in Europe, working for one of the greatest managers ever. It's going to be very tough to get to that level. I'm sure the academy staff are very proud of any player who goes on to the start of their career, whatever level that is.

'It's stages. Everybody's pathway is different. There isn't really a set one. You can be a youth-team player one year, then you can be fast-tracked. Phil Foden was a first-year scholar and was dropped into the first team. He missed out being a second-year scholar, effectively, and didn't really play under-23s. There are other examples of players who went through under-18s, under-23s, then first team, or under-23s then out on loan. There are many different pathways to a career. What we're trying to do as a club is get as many players through to the first team as we can. A career is a career, and some go a different way. There is a real responsibility to get these lads a career first and foremost, ideally with us, but elsewhere if not.'

Scott Sellars, Wolverhampton Wanderers' academy manager, takes Taylor's line of thinking one step further. As explored in earlier chapters, many clubs now take a holistic approach to development, focusing on moulding aspects of the individual beyond the pitch as well as on it, equipping them for a life in or out of the game. As such, Sellars believes he and his staff can feel content with a job well done if their players go on to find success and happiness in other walks of life. 'I view success off two things: players in the first team making their debuts, and players playing first-team football somewhere else,' he begins. 'So we may incur a fee, a value, or even if we let him go, he has a career in football. That is success.

'Also, a boy goes to university in America, gets a degree, and is successful in whatever he does. A boy could become an accountant; a boy could become a doctor – they're all successes. The key success will always be about first-team players, but we want to develop good people as well. I think it's about developing everything.'

At the end of a journey that began at eight years old or younger, through all the selection processes they faced along the way, surviving the cut year after year, and as carefully managed as their development might have been in order to get them ready for top-level first-team football, sometimes it's all still not quite enough. Often, that final leap toward grasping the long-held dream rests on quirks of timing and pure luck.

'It's not easy for a manager,' Issott sympathises. 'If you lose six games in a month, you're sacked. It's not easy for young players to gain a manager's trust. A lot of the time, it happens when there's nowhere else to turn.

'It's when talent meets opportunity. They're the two things you need.'

The unfortunate reality is that only the former is ever in bountiful supply.

CHAPTER THIRTEEN

STAYING THE JOURNEY

WE END WHERE we began: across a picnic table from Tony Whelan, Manchester United's assistant academy director, on a bracing afternoon in October 2020. We find the youth coach of more than thirty years in reflective mood. 'I'm not sure I would be a footballer today,' he says, 'because people were patient with me.

'I was a late developer. They say football is a late-development sport. If it's a late-development sport, I wonder why we've got kids in academies and in programmes at clubs as young as six and seven and eight.

'I'm so grateful that I still had the joys of childhood when I was a kid. I spent loads of time with my mates. I went to my own birthday parties. I went to watch Man United and Man City. When I look back at my childhood, it was just so much fun and joyous. I never felt any real stress when I was a schoolboy player, even when I went to Man United. There's a danger at the moment, with all the systems and the ways that it's going with academies and the structure of it, I think a lot of the joy has been taken away in that sense.'

Many of the coaches and academy managers interviewed for this book agree with Whelan, that clubs are able to sign children to their academies at too young an age. Privately, they have expressed that they'd welcome the minimum age at which children can be contracted to academies to be raised as high as twelve. But the Premier League's own research has found that almost half of the homegrown players aged twenty-three or under currently playing in the division were registered with an academy before their tenth birthday. That statistic will be seen by clubs and the game's policy-shapers as vindication of the *Charter for Quality*'s ruling back in the late 1990s that players could be tied to an academy from the under-9s level. Whelan is unconvinced. He believes what he terms as 'protecting childhood' is football's biggest blind spot when it comes to youth development.

'It's as clear to me as the nose on my face,' he says. 'When you look at the number of young people going from club to club – and I'm not talking about seventeen, eighteen, which is still young, by the way – I ask the question: what are we doing? We've got six-, seven-, eight-year-old boys going to major Premier League clubs on a regular basis. Add ten years, they're only going to be eighteen. I'm not sure that's really healthy for anybody, because the journey is so long.'

He glazes over as he recalls a scene he witnessed days earlier while jogging past a local high school as the children were leaving to go home. 'They were bouncing out,' he says. Backpacks on, ties slung loose and shirts untucked, some congregated near the road with mischief in their eyes, others gathered on benches. The older boys carried an insouciant swagger as they approached the girls of their year, believing themselves coolness personified. Kids being kids. Whelan was reminded of the youngsters he has worked with over the years and the sacrifices they have made. 'Should they have to give that up?' he asks. 'Would you want to give up your childhood? The attrition rate is so high. Do you want to take a chance on missing out on your childhood? Not everybody makes it.

'It's not easy, given the numbers. That's another issue, the number of kids in academies. I'm astonished by the numbers. You've got players that are registered in an age group with twenty other kids, and there's only one match on a Saturday or Sunday. How are these kids going to get football? I'm training, and I'm going up and down motorways all week. I might be going to and fro, ten hours in a car a week for one game of football at best. I'm not sure we're getting that right at all. I think we're a long way from getting it right. And when you look at the UN Convention, the Rights of the Child [an international human-rights treaty that sets out the civil, political, economic, social, health and cultural rights of children], and you look at some of the clauses in there in terms of development, in terms of exploitation, trafficking and all of that – in that context, I think it's worrying. Very close to the line.'

Whelan's decades in youth football have not numbed him to the mass heartbreak it has made intrinsic. Although most of his peers cannot trace a history in the game back as far as he does, the vast majority of academy coaches were once hopeful young footballers themselves, many of whom will have fallen short of their ultimate ambition. It might be five decades in the past, but Whelan has never forgotten the hurt he felt when he left United as a young player. The emotions are vivid and real the instant he casts his mind back, and they are at the root of his concerns for the way the academy system is progressing, each year churning through young lives by the hundred.

'In my case, I know what it feels like,' he says. 'I left Man United when I was twenty. It was one of the saddest days of my life. I can still remember it like it was yesterday. I don't really drink, but I remember going to visit my friend in Manchester, distraught, and not remembering where I was the next day. I think that's only happened to me once in my life. That's how bad it was for me, so I have a lot of empathy for young players because of that. I was gutted when I left Manchester United. I've never forgotten that experience, so I know how it feels.

'A kid gets released from Man United at sixteen, does that mean they're not going to be a footballer? If the young person wants it to be that way, then all right. But maybe he doesn't. These young people need encouragement; they need a lift. They don't need to be told they're not good enough at this age and younger. That's what the system is doing. A young kid comes into a youth development system at nine and ten, they're only on one-year contracts. After one year, they're on their bike. They go somewhere else. Is that acceptable? I don't think it is. If you want to sign a young kid, sign him and trust in him and believe in him and go with him. Stay the journey.

'In childhood, if you've been at a football club seven, eight, nine years, you've formed some strong connections with people, not just with your peers but also staff. It's quite traumatic. When you start to think quite deeply about these things, you're not a human being if it doesn't tug at your heartstrings. I think sometimes, because there are so many young players in the system and so many clubs and everybody's got an academy, that gets lost amongst it all.'

Huw Jennings, Fulham's academy director, brings a unique perspective to the debate surrounding the age at which academies should be able to sign children. He first garnered a reputation as one of the most respected developers of talent in the country while Southampton's academy director between 2001 and 2006, overseeing the graduation of Gareth Bale and Theo Walcott, among others, from the club's youth ranks. He then spent two years working as the Premier League's head of youth development before taking his current position at Fulham. But Jennings had a career before his involvement in football. For twelve years, he was a secondary-school teacher in Oxfordshire. Informed by his experience within the world of education, he sees the merits of allowing young children to be coached at elite academies, although the formality of the current structure, he feels, is ripe for change.

'Where I sit with it is,' Jennings says, 'with the "golden years of learning" [from age six to twelve], we need to ensure that the expertise of professional clubs works alongside these youngsters of this age, but I would do away with the competitive games element. This systematised games on a weekend, where you're constantly pitched up against another professional club – I would have a mixed economy. The mixed economy would allow those players in those ages to play with their peers, because I think that's important. I think that's important from a socialising aspect, from a fun aspect, from a learning aspect. But it's also important because it takes away that notion that you're a member of a professional football club where you're on a pathway to stardom.

'I think that's where we need now to tread a more middle line, getting the benefits from the highly skilled professionals working in the Foundation Phase. Kids who come into contact with those professionals really benefit from their wisdom and their skills, so we mustn't lose that. But nor should we undermine the natural element of the child's journey through this period – which, incidentally, should include access to other activities; other sports activities, other non-academic learning opportunities. If we can come up with a mixed economy of that type, I think we can find a sweet spot.'

Rather than academies shrinking in scope to focus on fewer players and higher age groups, an ideal to which Whelan and others would subscribe, Jennings is of the belief that further expansion might instead be required. There will come a day, he suggests, when there is a greater degree of collaboration between boys' and girls' football and provisions for those who conform to neither gender. I think in ten years' time you will have one academy that hosts both elements [boys and girls] up to eighteen, twenty-one,' he says, 'that there will be parity for girls and boys.

'At some point, we are going to have a young person who will want to play in the boys' programme who will declare themselves as either gender neutral or potentially as an alternative gender. At the moment, the rules for the Premier League don't permit that and they desperately need updating. That's the world we're in. As the organisers of the game, that's where we should be ensuring we facilitate it. Why shouldn't girls' academy programmes have the same parity? OK, the investment on the boys' side reflects the finances of the game, and that will continue for the time being, but you can certainly strive for parity. A real step change would be: the professional club's academy is a boys' and girls' academy.'

Speaking from his home office due to Covid lockdown measures, Jennings leans back in his chair as he ponders his vision for the future of football academies. 'I want to challenge the youth-development movement to ensure that we always have the needs of the individual at the forefront of our mind,' he says, highlighting an area in which Fulham have been seen as pioneering, having de-emphasised the importance of results within their academy teams at all ages, instead focusing on the specific developmental needs of each player. 'That element has improved. We're less team-focused. We're more focused on the needs of the individual. But I think there's still a long way to go with that. If you're not careful, you do find that there's a bit of a reverting to type sometimes for individuals in the game, where the performance or the results of a team matter more than the development of the individual.'

Jennings is concerned, also, by the chasm between under-23s football, the highest youth level, and the senior game. 'For some, they don't need it,' he says. 'Phil Foden didn't need it. They trained him consistently with the first team at Manchester

City and that was the stepping stone that he has needed. A number of others didn't have loans. Mason Greenwood didn't, Marcus Rashford didn't, and others. For some, a loan experience is important and is beneficial. It's a mixed economy. We need to continue to develop that mixed economy. I would be really pleased, not least because of the Brexit position, if we were to have more formalised opportunities to link with clubs. Why couldn't Fulham have a relationship with Crawley Town that enables us, without making the Football League anti-competitive, to have a closer liaison with Crawley Town? Those incremental things. I don't think there's a magic bullet here that's going to change and help the top end of an academy seamlessly integrate with the bottom end of a first-team environment. I think there are lots of incremental gains that are going to be needed as we progress.'

On balance, though, Jennings feels, while improvement must be a continual aim, that the English academy system has made healthy advancements over the last decade. The quality and number of players being produced is now of a level comparable to any nation. That, he believes, is worthy of positive reflection. 'I think the first thing to say is it's absolutely terrific to see the youth-development movement in academies has managed to develop a programme where the standard of individual player has improved immensely,' he says. 'I don't think standards have ever been higher. Standards of individual performance and coaching calibre. The support networks, the welfare, player-care support component, the professionalism of the sports science programme – standards have been raised immeasurably.

'I go back to the moniker that was applied to British players – "You're all right physically, but you're crap technically," type of thing. I think we've absolutely dispelled that myth. I thought it was always a myth. We've dispelled it on the back of some very, very good work, hard work, over a long period of time, a sustained twenty-year period. That has to continue. Until we have a dynasty of highly able players in the professional game and their respective nations, the work will always be necessary.'

Whelan echoes Jennings's sentiments about the strides youth development in English football has made in recent years, praising the 'wonderful things going on in academies'. Whelan was sixteen before he first travelled anywhere by aeroplane, he says, on a trip to Switzerland for a youth tournament with United. Now, boys as young as nine and ten within the club's academy travel the world for competitions. And the vast improvement in facilities, the science behind the prevention and treatment of injuries, workload balancing and coaching methods have all contributed to the emergence of a steady stream of highly talented players from English academies. The continuation of these advancements will ensure the production lines that churned out the likes of England internationals Marcus Rashford, Phil Foden, Jadon Sancho, Mason Mount and Trent Alexander-Arnold will grow yet more prolific. 'I think we have to celebrate that,' Whelan says.

On matters of welfare and wellbeing, though, he feels football still falls short.

'We've just got to work a lot harder at the other stuff.'

ACKNOWLEDGEMENTS

I DON'T RECALL the exact moment the idea for this book came to me. I do remember, though, that at the very beginning I doubted it was viable. It was only as I stood on the grass of the outer training pitch at Crystal Palace's academy, on a bizarrely warm and sunny February afternoon, waiting for an under-18s training session to begin, that I thought, 'OK, this might be doable.'

The reason for my doubt was that I feared I'd be unable to gain the access to the inner workings of the academy world that I needed. From the outside, I perceived football clubs to be guarded of their academies, reluctant to open their doors unless it was on their terms, when they were sure of a positive press. And that may be the case. But I quickly found that the people on the inside, the ones whose feet touch the turf – the coaches, the players, the support staff – are proud of their work, passionate about what they do, and keen to tell their stories.

Palace were the first club I visited. In the end, I travelled the length and breadth of the country for two years, spending time at a dozen or so academies at various levels and meeting with scores more people whose expertise and insight fill these pages. So to everyone who gave me their time and their wisdom, I owe the deepest thanks.

I'd also like to thank Pete Burns and Polaris Publishing for believing in this book and bringing it to life. The space and freedom I was given to finish writing and reporting and the responsiveness I was met with whenever I needed it made this project infinitely smoother and more enjoyable.

A huge thank-you, too, goes to Martin Greig of BackPage Press, who was so incredibly kind and giving of his time in providing sage feedback and helping mould and improve both my proposal and manuscript.

Thanks, also, to everyone listed here, who either opened their contacts book to me and helped arrange one of the many, many interviews that formed the basis of this book or offered advice along the way: Danny Taylor, David Conn, Jamie Jackson, Simon Austin, Andy Kelly, Alex Rowan, Michael Beale, Jo Tongue, Gavin Blackwell, Jim White, Steven Chicken, David Threlfall-Sykes, Andy Walker, Carmelo Misfud, Darren Bentley, Luke Thompson, Sam McGuire, Frank Smith, Ian Brewster, Tony Mount, George Bowyer, Ciaran Kelly. And to Jasmine Baba for help with transcribing one of the longer interviews.

There is no person more crucial to this book's existence than my wonderful, encouraging and ever-understanding partner, Sophie. Your support is the foundation upon which not only this book but my entire career is built. Thank you – again – for always offering an empathetic ear. For enabling me to find the space in our lives as parents to see through this project. For reigniting my belief in it whenever it threatened to fade. For everything.

And finally, thanks to Dylan, our little boy. Thank you for putting up with Daddy taking phone calls when we were at the park and doing Zoom interviews when you were trying to watch *Hey Duggee*. Thank you for taking naps just long enough to allow me to squeeze out an extra paragraph or two. And thank you for being the brightest, funniest, most joyous person I know.

INDEX

POLARIS
PUBLISHING